THE LAST
QUEENS
OF
EGYPT

THE LAST QUEENS OF EGYPT

OF

EGYPT

SALLY-ANN ASHTON

PEARSON
Longman

PEARSON EDUCATION LIMITED

Head Office:
Edinburgh Gate
Harlow CM20 2JE
Tel: +44 (0)1279 623623
Fax: +44 (0)1279 431059

London Office:
128 Long Acre
London WC2E 9AN
Tel: +44 (0)20 7447 2000
Fax: +44 (0)20 7447 2170
Website: www.history-minds.com

———————————

First edition published in Great Britain in 2003

© Pearson Education Limited 2003

The right of Sally-Ann Ashton to be identified as Author
of this Work has been asserted by her in accordance
with the Copyright, Designs and Patents Act 1988.

ISBN 0 582 77210 9

British Library Cataloguing in Publication Data
A CIP catalogue record for this book can be obtained from the British Library

Library of Congress Cataloging in Publication Data
A CIP catalog record for this book can be obtained from the Library of Congress

10 9 8 7 6 5 4 3 2 1

Set by Fakenham Photosetting Limited, Fakenham, Norfolk
Printed and bound in China

The Publishers' policy is to use paper manufactured from sustainable forests.

CONTENTS

For Evelyn Foster Ashton

PREFACE

This book is intended for the general reader and, as a consequence, references have been kept to a minimum. However, a full source and reading list is provided at the back of the book and where comments or ideas are those of people other than the author their publications are mentioned in the text. It is also hoped that the book will serve as a general background introduction to undergraduate students who may be familiar with only one part of the Ptolemaic character and that it will provide a general introduction to aspects of Ptolemaic Egypt.

The reason for the paucity of publications on Egyptian queens when compared to kings is probably partly on account of the difficulty of finding relevant information. Personalities are virtually impossible to determine, the closest we can come is to consider the achievements of individuals and their presentation, which means that it is often necessary to rely heavily on archaeological evidence. Cleopatra and her ancestors often received bad press, usually at the hands of Roman authors and for this reason the present publication attempts to look beyond this bias in order to obtain a more rounded understanding of the role played by the Ptolemaic royal women.

ACKNOWLEDGEMENTS

I would like to thank Frances Nutt for providing an inspirational image, illustrated in the Introduction. I am extremely grateful to Ian Blair, Lucilla Burn and Clare Pickersgill for patiently reading through the text and for their suggestions on the organisation of chapters; to Wolfram Grajetzki for sharing his thoughts on early dynastic queens and for his many other comments on the first draft of Chapter 1, and to Stephen Quirke for discussing several issues arising from this chapter. I would like to express a special thanks to Susan Walker for her advice on the structure and content of several chapters; the book is an easier read as a consequence. Any errors within the text remain my own.

   I am extremely grateful to the following museums for permission to publish photographs of objects within their collections: the Fitzwilliam Museum, Cambridge (Figure 2); the Ny Carlsberg Glyptotek, Copenhagen (Figures 22, 23); the British Museum, London (Figure 5); the Petrie Museum of Egyptian Archaeology, University College, London (Figure 28); the Musée Royal du Mariemont, Mariemont (Figures 8, 11, 20); the Metropolitan Museum of Art, New York (Figure 24); Vatican Museums (Figure 16); and the Kunsthistorisches Museum, Vienna (Figure 25). I am also grateful to the following individuals for their help in obtaining permissions: Mr Ahmed Abd el Fattah, Professor Mamdouh M. el Damaty, Ms Clare Derricks, Dr Morgens Jørgensen, Ms Ilse Jung, Mr Ivor Kerslake, Ms Sally Macdonald and Dr Mette Moltesen.

In some instances the publishers have been unable to trace the owners of copyright material, and would appreciate any information that would enable them to do so.

Finally I would like to thank Casey Mein of Pearson Education for suggesting this project and for her patience in seeing it through to fruition, and also my in-house editor, Melanie Carter.

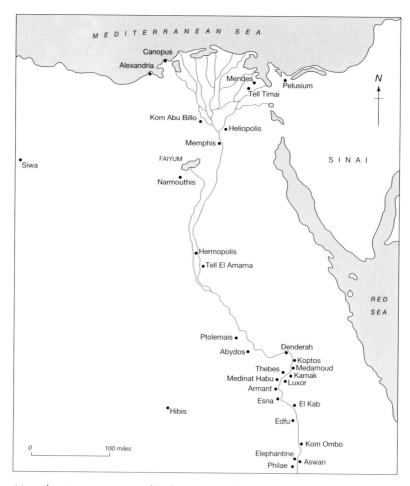

Map showing some sites of Ptolemaic royal patronage

Introduction

Cleopatra VII is a major contender for the title of Egypt's most famous queen; she and her ancestors were Macedonian Greek by descent and, as we shall see, maintained their links to the classical world, but they were also enthusiastic rulers of Egypt and supporters of Egyptian culture. There were in fact six queens with the name Cleopatra; confusingly, however, the best known is now distinguished from her predecessors by being identified as Cleopatra VII. Such mistakes are typical for a period that has caused confusion among modern scholars because of its dual persona. For those who take the time to consider the two faces of the Ptolemaic character, the reward is an insight not only into a complex but well-planned co-existence of two ancient cultures but, in terms of Egyptian history, also into profound developments in language, art and religion at a time that is often considered to be its twilight years.

This period saw an increase in the amount of power held by Egyptian royal women and developments in their political and religious roles. For the first time Egyptian artists, faced with the challenge of representing these modifications, developed new ways in which to represent the royal women. Some former queens of Egypt, however, had already enjoyed the

Figure 1 (By Frances Nutt. Copyright and reproduced courtesy of Frances Nutt. The Petrie Museum of Egyptian Archaeology, University College London, UC 14521. The Greco-Roman Museum, Alexandria 3227.

powers invested in previous queens, as regents, goddesses and even pharaohs. This factor is important for our understanding of the promotion of the earliest Ptolemaic queens to a status beyond that ever seen in Greece, and is apparent in the developments of the Ptolemaic royal image from the third century BC.

In Greek history the death of Cleopatra VII marks the end of the Hellenistic age. This period began after the death of Alexander the Great in 323 BC, when his vast kingdom was divided among his generals. It was a time when countries fell under the control and influence of Greeks and Greek rulers. It is also a time that saw an increase in the political role of women in the Greek world, and the Ptolemaic queens were without doubt the most prominent royal women of the Hellenistic period.

There is no one ancient image that is truly representative of the character of the Ptolemaic royal women, nor is there a representation that can allow us, as modern viewers, to share the impact that the appearance of the queens in Egypt in the fourth century BC would have made. As a modern audience we are as familiar with ancient Egyptian images as we are with those that were adopted and used in western art. How, then, can we understand the impact of the development of the presentation of the Ptolemaic queens, or how either Greek immigrant or native Egyptian reacted to these alien figures. The modern image illustrated in Figure 1 is probably the closest that the modern viewer can come to fully comprehending the way in which the queens presented themselves. It is a hybrid of styles and periods that together form the essence of what it was to be a queen in Ptolemaic Egypt. This image is particularly pertinent for the last queen of Egypt. Was she Macedonian or Egyptian? Both Greece and Egypt lay claim to her. Was she black? Was she beautiful? Did she really have such a large nose? It is difficult to imagine the same questions being asked of a king, and yet these are the types of question that are by far the greatest preoccupation with Cleopatra today. This book will not attempt to determine the physical appearance of the Ptolemaic royal women, because the stylised forms of image do not allow us to do so. What they do permit is a greater insight into 300 years of inspiration that influenced the last and most famous Ptolemaic queen

NOTE ON TEXT

The Pre-Ptolemaic Chronology is taken from I. Shaw (ed.), *Oxford History of Ancient Egypt* (2000). The Ptolemaic Chronology is after G. Hölbl, *A History of the Ptolemaic Empire* (2001).

CHAPTER 1

Role models

The ideological and religious roles of Egyptian queens

In a world that was dominated by the male pharaoh, it is often difficult to comprehend fully the roles of Egyptian queens. A pharaoh would have a number of queens, but the most important would be elevated to 'principal wife'. Titles that were adopted by queens often indicated a political or social as well as religious standing. There are two modern publications that list titles of the principal members of the royal family. The first is a compendium of the titles and names of Egyptian rulers that was published in 1916 by the French Egyptologist Gauthier, in five volumes, and called *Livre des Rois*. More recently Troy explored the roles of queens and the meaning of their titles, presenting an interpretation of what it was to be an Egyptian queen, and various other publications, such as Robins' *Women in Ancient Egypt,* include a chapter on queenship, considering some of the better-known royal women. There has been one major and notable exhibition on Egyptian women, which has also included some queens but when we consider how many individual publications and special exhibitions there have been on pharaohs of Egypt there is somewhat of an imbalance. Part of the reason for this lack of interest in Egyptian queens is that, compared to their male consorts, we know little about them, either historically or in terms of their presentation. What evidence we have reveals not one, but several important roles that the Egyptian royal women fulfilled. One important point to note is that there is no word in Egyptian for queen. In the Ptolemaic period the Greek word *Bassilisa* (which translates as queen) was used for the royal women. The term 'queen' will be used in an Egyptian context here for convenience and ease of reading, but in Egyptian terms, as we shall see from the various roles of royal women, it is not an easily definable concept.

The mother of the pharaoh

Without doubt, one of the most important aspects of queenship was the role of mother of the pharaoh, and in this capacity the queens of Egypt became associated with the goddess Isis, who was mother of Horus, who was in turn represented on earth by the living ruler. Neithhotep was the first named Egyptian queen of the 1st Dynasty (3000–2890 BC) and her name appears in association with two early kings, Aha and Djer, to whom she is thought to have acted as regent. Queen Meritneith was also associated with king Djer, king Djet and king Den, of whom she was possibly the mother. On seal from Abydos, and now in the Petrie Museum of Egyptian Archaeology, Meritneith appears as 'king's mother'. Her importance is illustrated by the size of her tomb at Abydos, which is equal to those of the kings. That a woman was able to hold such a position in the 1st Dynasty is important for our understanding of the early role of Egyptian royal women and the continuity of association with the male rulers.

A 6th Dynasty statue, dating to the reign of Pepi II (2278–2184 BC) and now in the Brooklyn Museum of Art, clearly illustrates the role of the queen as 'king's mother'. The queen, Ankhnesmeryre II, sits with her son, Pepi II, on her knees; on the base of the statue the queen is described as 'mother of the king of Upper and Lower Egypt, the god's daughter, who is revered, beloved of Khnum'. Pepi II was about 6 years of age when he succeeded to the throne and his mother, Ankhnesmeryre II, enjoyed a prominent position, appearing with and associating herself with the king by means of her titles; thus justifying her role through the male members of the dynasty. This position of mother and son was later adopted for representations of Isis with her son Horus. Such images are extremely common from the New Kingdom to the Ptolemaic period, and are also adopted by Romano-Egyptian artists in the first century AD. The concept and image are not dissimilar to the later Christian Madonna and child.

The phenomenon of a former queen of a pharaoh being promoted as mother of a new pharaoh from the time of the 1st Dynasty demonstrates that from early Egyptian history there were defined roles for royal women. Indeed, when she outlived her consort and was replaced in that primary role by the new queen of the new pharaoh, the queen mother occupied a recognised position within the royal court. In many cases the role of a royal woman was dependent upon the ruler, hence the titles 'king's mother', 'king's sister' and 'king's wife'. None of these positions seems to have been fixed and there are huge discrepancies between individual women, sometimes as a result of a poor historical record, but in other cases because the individual stands out in terms of a religious or political role. The same is true of the Ptolemaic queens, and for each category of this period there is an earlier role model. In some instances, as we shall see, Egyptian artists refer back to images that were made 1000 years previously in order to distinguish between the various roles that the Ptolemaic royal women fulfilled.

Divine queens and their symbols of status

There are two methods of tracking the ideology of queenship: firstly, through the study of images and attributes and, secondly, by the titles they adopted. In addition to being linked to the king, queens were also associated with gods or goddesses, either through their titles, for example 'daughter of Geb', or in a role that linked them to a specific deity such as 'god's wife of Amun'. It is important to explore these links further to obtain a clear understanding of later associations between the Ptolemaic queens and divinities, and indeed their own divine status. In most instances associations were intended to elevate the status of the individual, and although this is true for all periods it seems to reach almost impossible heights during the reign of Cleopatra III, when the queen herself was worshipped as a goddess in her own right and honoured with five out of nine of the eponymous cults of Alexandria, as a goddess in the dynastic cult with her consort, and also as the personification of Isis.

The status of a queen was marked by the uraeus or cobra, which they wore on their brow. The uraeus was a protective symbol, initially worn on the crowns or headdresses of the pharaoh, and, by association, the queen of Egypt; it was associated with the sun god Ra and usually appeared as a single figure. It has been suggested that the uraeus may also have been linked to female deities and the solar myth, particularly with Hathor as the eye of Ra. From the 6th Dynasty the queen sometimes wears a vulture head with a cap depicting the wings and tail. This particular symbol is usually associated with divine images, and appears on certain occasions on representations of royal women, certainly until the end of the New Kingdom. Its use in the Ptolemaic period is not as straightforward and will be discussed further in Chapter 5. The cobra and vulture also represent the goddesses of Upper and Lower Egypt and as a hieroglyph the cobra was used as a determinative for goddesses.

However, from the time of the 18th Dynasty (1550–1069 BC), some queens wore a double uraeus. The earliest appearance of the double form was on the statues of an 18th Dynasty queen, called Isis, who was the wife of Thutmose II (1492–1479) and mother of Thutmose III (1479–1425 BC); it is used in conjunction with the title 'mother of the king'. The double form of the motif is most consistently found on images of another 18th Dynasty queen, Tiye, who was the consort and principal wife of Amenhotep III (1390–1352 BC), and mother of Amenhotep IV, who is perhaps more familiar as Akhenaten, the heretic pharaoh (1352–1336 BC). On the double uraeus of Tiye, one cobra wears the crown of Upper Egypt and the other the crown of Lower Egypt; on some of her statues the cobras are divided by a vulture, thus illustrating her divine status as well as that of queen of the two kingdoms of Egypt. When Amenhotep IV came to the throne his mother was still alive, and so to distinguish between the mother of the king and the wife of the king, the latter, Nefertiti, initially wore a single uraeus on her brow. It was not long, however, before Nefertiti was shown with the double uraeus, although interestingly only on a small number of representations, perhaps indicating a specific role or event in the royal court. The uraei of Nefertiti are never shown with the crowns of Egypt, but the queen did adopt the title 'lady of the two lands' – in other words, Upper and Lower Egypt. Nefertiti's uraei, and indeed those of her successor Meritaten, are adorned with sun-disks and cow's horns. The double uraeus appears again on images of the 19th Dynasty queen and daughter of Ramesses II (1279–1213 BC), Meritamun. The Third Intermediate Period queen Shepenwepet I, who also wore the sun-disk and cow's horns – perhaps stressing a link between the uraeus and Hathor and the eye of Ra – was chosen to be 'god's wife' by her father Osorkon II (874–850 BC). This associated the women with the god Amun and elevated their status to that of a god's consort. In this role they are shown with a vulture headdress, often in the embrace of the god. In contrast, the 25th Dynasty queen Amenirdas, who ruled in the eighth century BC, wore simply the double cobras, but also on occasion the vulture headdress, stressing her personal divinity. Like Shepenwepet I, Amenirdas held the title of 'god's wife'.

Because of the discrepancies in both titles and attributes which are associated with the double form of cobra, it is probably fair to conclude that it was used as a means of distinguishing a particular royal female, usually the principal wife, from others in the royal court. The later association with the god Amun is of particular relevance for the motif's reappearance in the Ptolemaic period and was probably used here to stress the divine link between queen and god. The doubling of a recognised attribute is a clever way of highlighting an individual or portraying the individual in a specific role. One has to remember that Egyptian kings had more than one wife, and also that the mother was often still alive on his succession to the throne. Traditional artistic and ideological canons limited the variations upon a single theme, and so artists – and probably priests, in the role of advisers – were forced to turn to familiar symbols by which to express themselves or, more to the point, to allow the image to be readable.

The Amarna royal women as forerunners of the Ptolemaic queens

The women of the Amarna period were in many respects closest to those of the Ptolemaic period because of the changes in the role of both pharaoh and royal wife, which had begun during the reign of Amenhotep III and queen Tiye. As previously noted, Tiye played both a supportive and active role in the presentation of the royal family and was distinguished from other royal women by her double uraeus and vulture headdress. In addition to Amenhotep IV, who later became Akhenaten, Tiye gave birth to four daughters of whom we have a record: Sitamun, whose name translates as 'daughter of Amun'; Henut taneb, who has a title meaning 'mistress of all lands', and is shown as a goddess on the colossal statue of the family from Medinat Habu, wearing a vulture headdress; Isis, who was obviously named after the goddess and who also adopted the title 'king's wife'; and Nebet ah, who was also named from a title meaning 'lady of the palace'. Here, it becomes apparent why Tiye should wear the double uraeus: it is to distinguish her from her daughters. It was Tiye, however, who was to have a lasting impact on the next phase of royal history and indeed frequently appears in the historical record following the accession of her son, moving from the role of principal wife to that of king's mother.

The 1996 catalogue for the special exhibition, *The Royal Women of Amarna,* offers a comprehensive overview of the women from this period. It is, however, worth considering a synopsis of the women and their roles. Nefertiti's full name is Nefernefuraten-Nefertiti, meaning 'the perfect one of Aten's perfection', 'the beautiful one is here'. For her titles Nefertiti was described as 'sweet of love', 'lady of all of the women'; others associated her with Akhenaten, such as 'she is at the side of Akhenaten forever just as the heavens will endure, bearing that which is in it' and 'great wife of the king whom he loves'. She was also associated with gods 'daughter of Geb', and given more traditional titles such as 'mistress of the two lands'. Her role was, in many respects, similar to that awarded to the early Ptolemaic queens. Nefertiti was not, however, Akhenaten's only wife: the ruler also appeared with a woman named Kiya.

Nefertiti and Akhenaten had six daughters together. Some scholars have suggested that the king married at least one because of her title of 'king's chief wife', her position on relief representations, which is closest to her father and also because her name and image eventually replaced those of Kiya. Another of the sisters, Ankhesenpaaten, was also possibly married to Akhenaten, and was later the wife of Tutankhamun. Her character is perhaps reflected in the request that she wrote, following Tutankhamun's death, to a Hittite ruler asking for a suitable consort to be sent to her, with whom she could rule. From documentary evidence we know of other wives of the Akhenaten, whose names appear in documents but who were probably not depicted in sculptural representations. Here, Nefertiti and their daughters prevailed.

This observation is at least partly due to the manner of worshipping the Aten, or light of the sun-disk, during the Amarna period, which could only be accessed through the royal couple Akhenaten and Nefertiti. As a consequence of this change in the theology of ancient Egyptian religion, the queen and her consort appear on all relief representations worshipping the Aten. When compared to other Egyptian royal scenes, the Amarna period produced unusual groupings, which show the closeness of the royal family, illustrated by an unfinished gem in the Fitzwilliam Museum, where the royal couple embrace, their daughters at

Figure 2 *An unfinished gem showing Akhenaten and Nefertiti and their daughters embracing. (Fitzwilliam Museum Cambridge EGA.4606.1943; copyright and reproduced with permission of The Fitzwilliam Museum.)*

their sides (Figure 2). It has been suggested that Nefertiti took the name 'the perfect one of the Aten's perfection' before the royal court was moved to Akhetaten or Tell el-Amarna, which is the modern Arabic name for the site. If this is the case, then Nefertiti may have been instrumental in one of the most innovative developments in the religion of ancient Egypt – indeed, not until Christianity arrived would such dramatic changes be seen again. There is, however, possibly more to Nefertiti's role than chief wife and mediator of the Aten. Some scholars believe that Nefertiti became co-regent with Akhenaten and indeed outlived him, changing her name, which would explain its disappearance from the historical record. She appeared on the corner of the sarcophagus of Akhenaten as a protective goddess wearing the double uraeus, but given the status of her predecessor, Tiye, during her lifetime and her own elevated status, such an appearance, while still living, would have been acceptable. There is considerable documentary evidence to support the idea of a co-regency but some scholars remain sceptical of both the identity of the female and indeed if there ever was a co-ruler.

Certainly, of all of the Amarna family, two women – Tiye and Nerfertiti, the two principal wives – are the most similar to their Ptolemaic counterparts. Both queens, as noted, were distinguished from other members of the female royal house by their attributes, in the case of the double uraeus, and also for the number of representations either as part of the king's presentation or alone. The queens also appear with their off-spring, thus forming a family alliance and promoting their daughters from an early age. In the case of Nefertiti, the queen's image was as carefully planned as that of her consort. The famous bust of Nefertiti from Tell el-Amarna, and now in the Egyptian Museum, Berlin, is a sculptors' model that was found in a royal workshop; it was abandoned by the artists when they left the city early in the reign of Tutankhamun. The existence of such a model suggests a careful attention to detail and to the dissemination of the queen's image. For the most part the images of Nefertiti follow the same three stages that were identified by

Aldred: grossly exaggerated, less exaggerated and then idealised. Nefertiti's early images are masculine in that they copy that of Akhenaten, and we find a parallel for this in the images of Cleopatra III which copy those of her sons, resulting in what appears at first sight to be a man in a woman's attire.

Late period royal women

Among the late Egyptian female rulers the closest parallels to the Ptolemaic queens are the 25th Dynasty women. This dynasty is often referred to as the Kushite, because the queens ruled in the kingdom of Kush, modern Sudan, and so like the Ptolemaic queens they were foreigners. Amenirdas I, the sister or half-sister of the ruler Piy (747–716 BC) was installed as the 'god's wife of Amun' at Thebes. Scholars believe that Amenirdas I was the aunt of Piya's successor and the family continuity of the role of 'god's wife' is expressed through her successor, Piya's sister Shepenwepet II.

Titles and power were often associated with a specific role, as illustrated by those adopted by Nitokret 'god's wife' of the 26th Dynasty, the daughter of Psammeticus I and Meketenusekht. Nitokret was called 'beloved of Amun; the daughter who is created by Atum; hand of the god; she who adores the god; first priestess of Amun, the one who pacifies Horus with her voice, sister of the king, daughter of the king and the female Horus'. Divine association was among the first Egyptian traditions adopted by the Ptolemies and for this reason the royal women were extremely useful in the promotion of the dynasty and so the pharaoh. The problem for the Ptolemaic men, however, was that by the second century BC the women started to believe in their own divinity and, as a consequence, political power.

Whether they were aware of their predecessors we cannot know. Manetho, the Egyptian historian working at the Mouseion in Alexandria, chronicled the Egyptian kings, but whether the young princesses were read stories of the powerful queens of Egypt must remain speculative. Cleopatra VII was well educated, as illustrated by her command of several languages, and during the Ptolemaic period there becomes an increasing closeness between the royal family and the Egyptian priests. The possible re-use of an Amarna statue at Karnak is suggestive, given the connection between the royal women who were 1000 years apart. The statue was found at the Karnak temple, close to the Roman chapel; it is now housed in the Karnak Museum. An 18th Dynasty date has been suggested for the original statue, which was much later inscribed with the cartouche of Cleopatra II. The representation is preserved from the abdomen to the lower thighs and only the last few characters of the cartouche have survived. More recently, scholars have suggested that is a Ptolemaic original rather than Amarna piece. At the very least the close visual association illustrates a link between the two periods, which is found elsewhere on non-royal terracotta representations.

There are only a few representations of royal women from the dynasties immediately preceding that of the Ptolemies, and many are associated with the role of god's wife rather than consort to the king. Comparatively speaking, however, the Ptolemaic period brought a renaissance for the female royal image.

Female pharaohs

It is interesting to note that not until the Ptolemaic period was there a tradition within a single dynasty of women with increased powers, except perhaps in the case of Tiye, Nefertiti and the daughters of Akhenaten. For such a development a dramatic change in status, indeed a change in Egyptian ideological tradition, was required and typically queens only ruled as a last resort at the end of a dynasty. The exception is Hatshepsut, who ruled part way through the 18th Dynasty. Such exceptions to the rule have prompted some scholars to suggest that an elevated status was partially dependent on the strength of a queen's personality rather than the prevailing political or social climate. In fact, we often have comparatively little information about queens compared to pharaohs, because their role does not require depiction in the same way as their consorts.

From the Old Kingdom comes a female for whom there is no contemporary evidence but who appears in the Turin canon, a list of kings that dates from the reign of Ramesses II. In the list Neithikret is called 'King of [Upper and] Lower Egypt' and according to the document she reigned before the 6th Dynasty ruler Pepi II. With the exception of the possible sole reign by Neithikret, it was not until the Middle Kingdom that a woman was promoted to regent or ruler, and the decision to represent a female pharaoh is indicative of the domination of men in this role. Sobeknefru was co-regent with Amenemhat III and/or Amenemhat IV at the end of the 12th Dynasty; and following the death of Amenemhat IV, Sobeknefru ruled as pharaoh of Egypt from 1777–1773 BC. As ruler she was shown wearing the traditional nemes head-cloth and kilt over the usual female attire, which is interesting on two accounts: firstly, her sex was indicated in her representations and, secondly, the conventions were such that the only way to show the pharaoh was in male clothes. Her titles were those of a male pharaoh.

The best-known female pharaoh is of course Hatshepsut who, as previously noted, unusually ruled in the middle of a dynasty (18th Dynasty), from 1473–1458 BC. Hatshepsut was the daughter of Thutmose I (c. 1504–1492 BC), the half-sister and wife of Thutmose II (c. 1492–1479 BC) and co-regent with Thutmose III (1479–1425 BC). Hatshepsut's reign is well documented by stelae, statuary and the building projects with which she was involved, the most famous of which is her mortuary temple at Deir el-Bahri on the west bank of Thebes. The documents studied by scholars illustrate Hatshepsut's promotion from 'god's wife' to regent for her nephew and stepson Thutmose III, to co-regent. She was shown, or chose to be represented, in the guise of a male pharaoh wearing the nemes head-cloth and kilt, but with breasts under a sheath-like traditional female dress. During her rule, her daughter by Thutmose II, Neferure, was given the role and title of 'god's wife', thus fulfilling an important role for her mother. Hatshepsut disappears from the record in the twentieth year of the reign of Thutmose III; 26 years later, during the final years of his reign, the king seems to have ordered the removal of the queen's names from monuments and statues, re-using many with a changed cartouche. Bryan, in *Mistress of the House*, an essay for the special exhibition, suggests that the son and successor of Thutmosis also joined in this damnation, most probably in order to ensure his own promotion as successor to the throne.

Attempts to seize the throne by ambitious royal women such as Tauseret, who was the principal wife of Sety II at the end of the 19th Dynasty (1200–1194 BC), were thwarted by powerful advisers within the court. Such men preferred to place an easily manipulated young male child on the throne than deal with the former king's wife. It is possible that the queen ruled as co-regent but she did not manage to elevate herself to the status of pharaoh and, as such, has more in common with the majority of the last queens of Egypt than with Sobeknefru or Hatshepsut. This story is similar to that of many of the Ptolemaic queens, some of whom ruled for brief periods alone but all of whom took, often not of their own will, a male consort.

Greek role models

There have been several modern studies of Hellenistic queens, the most notable by Macurdy in 1932, and a later discussion by Pomeroy as part of a more general study of Hellenistic women, first published in 1984, and reprinted with additions in 1990. Pomeroy notes that in a Greek context there was no public office of queen – in other words, there was no Hellenistic Greek equivalent to the defined role of Egyptian queen and it is difficult to find a role model as such from the Greek world. In Egypt the queen was either the consort or mother of the pharaoh. There were minor Egyptian queens, but even among the royal women the principal wife had a clearly defined role to play; this was not the case in the Greek world.

There were not Greek role models as there were Egyptian for the simple reason that Greek women did not typically play an active political role in society. On the margins of the Greek world there were exceptions to this rule, most notably and relevantly here in the wives of Philip II of Macedonia. Philip, who was Alexander the Great's father, married seven women, accumulating wives to cement political unions but never divorcing, probably, as Pomeroy notes, because to do so would have caused an international incident. As a consequence of this practice the Macedonian court was filled with women from many countries, who often brought their own traditions to their new life. Philip's wives were warriors and, as such, fought in battles and were buried in the tombs at Vergina (now in northern Greece) with items of military dress, such as greaves. Some of the wives were also politically astute. One of Philip's daughters, Cynane, even campaigned with him, fighting on the battlefield; she also threw herself into the political arena by arranging for her daughter to marry Alexander's half-brother and successor, Philip Arrhidaios. Perhaps the most notable and influential of the Macedonian women was Olympias, Alexander's mother, a woman who would have fulfilled the role of Egyptian mother of the pharaoh or principal wife with ease. Olympias fully embroiled herself in court politics and, following the death of Alexander the Great, was determined to get her younger son Philip IV, on the throne. In 317 BC, Olympias invaded Macedonia and was met by Eurydice, wife of Philip Arrhidaios, on the battlefield. Eurydice and her supporters surrendered to Olympias; Philip Arrhidaios was executed, along with many of his supporters, and Eurydice was forced to commit suicide. Like many of the Ptolemaic queens Olympias used her daughter, Cleopatra, Alexander's full sister, as a political pawn by sending her to one of Alexander's generals, Perdiccas, to be his wife. Olympias also courted deification, making the most of her son's elevated status, and her statue appeared in a small temple dedicated to Alexander and his family at Olympia in Greece. The main driving ambition for Olympias was the political position of her children and this was quite different to most of the Ptolemaic period, when self-preservation was usually higher on the agenda. Although it is certainly safe to say that Olympias' motive was probably closely related to her own personal need for authority, as a sort of matriarch she would have yielded considerable power.

CHAPTER 2

Egypt and the Ptolemies

Pharaohs and temples

The Ptolemies were not the first foreign pharaohs of Egypt, but they were arguably among the most enthusiastic advocates of Egyptian culture and, like many of those who have been converted to any cause, they promoted their newly found identity more voraciously than they might have done, had they descended from Egyptian kings. Their role model was, of course, Alexander the Great, who during his conquest of Egypt, which removed the second Persian dynasty, threw himself into the native Egyptian culture and showed an awareness of the traditions by making a treacherous journey across the desert to visit the Oracle of Ammon in the Oasis of Siwa. Alexander is depicted as pharaoh only once, at Karnak, but it is enough to show, firstly, Egypt's need for a pharaoh, both politically and ideologically, and secondly, Alexander's willingness to play this role.

The rulers tried their best to balance an active foreign policy with their rule of Egypt and for the third century BC succeeded, creating one of the most powerful of the Hellenistic kingdoms. During this time the rulers promoted themselves in territorial possessions such as Cyprus and Cyrenaica, in modern Libya, as Greek dynasts. Local craftsmen produced images that would have been familiar to the Greek communities in Egypt, and this observation implies a certain amount of control on behalf of the royal house, in the promotion of their official image. In Egypt, however, the rulers made an attempt to introduce Egyptian features to essentially Greek environments. The promotion of the god Sarapis is a perfect example of this clever policy. Sarapis was a Greek version of an existing Egyptian deity (Osiris-Apis), which was effectively the cult of the dead Apis bull. The bull was believed to be the living embodiment of the god Ptah, in other words a sort of ideological representative on earth. At some point, probably early in the reign of Ptolemy II, the Greek god, visually related to Zeus or Asklepios, was presented to the Greek communities and a Greek-style temple was built in Alexandria. At the doorway of the temple, however, were two colossal Egyptian sphinxes with the Egyptian portrait features of two early rulers. This practice is further illustrated by the movement of an obelisk from the abandoned site of Heliopolis to the new temple of Arsinoe II in Alexandria by Ptolemy II. In this way the early Ptolemies laid foundations that were not totally Hellenic, and the later rulers built upon these stones, more or less abandoning Greek images for those that showed them as Egyptian pharaohs but maintained the portrait features which the Greeks, both at home and abroad, could recognise.

As pharaohs the Ptolemies were the high priests of the gods and, as such, appeared on temple walls throughout Egypt making offerings to the Egyptian divine pantheon. They appeared where new temples or chapels were built and so, by financing these building programmes, the rulers were promoted as pharaohs among the gods of Egypt. These projects range from additional gateways in what can only be seen as a rather cheap way of promoting themselves over their predecessors, either immediate or past, to large-scale temple buildings. The early Ptolemies targeted areas that had been started by the last Egyptian dynasty (30th Dynasty) by means of linking themselves to this tradition. They also completed projects that had been started during the two periods of Persian occupation, perhaps as a means of celebrating Alexander's victory. In this way the new dynasty was able to associate itself with Egypt's past, while stamping its own unique mark on the Egyptian tradition.

Ptolemy I targeted the Delta, only going as far south as the Faiyum, which is still technically in Lower Egypt. The only exception to this observation was the Greek city called Ptolemais, which was established in Middle Egypt. There were of course references to the ruler at Karnak, but no large scale projects have been recognised to date. Under his successor, Ptolemy II, royal patronage spread, with temples as far south as Philae, where a gateway was attached to the pylon of the 30th Dynasty ruler Nectanebo II. The scenes that decorate the gate are executed in purely pharaonic style; they show Philadelphos offering to the gods, with Isis appearing on several registers receiving gifts from the king. Arsinoe II, his sister-wife, appears twice, once as consort to Isis where she receives a lotus from the king and again with Nephthys, who was the sister of Isis. Arsinoe, who was deified posthumously, can be seen on the walls with two more-established Egyptian goddesses.

The second building phase at Philae was the main temple which Philadelphos dedicated to Isis. Only the main chapel was built by the king; the hypostyle hall was a later edition by Ptolemy VIII Euergetes II. Although the outside of the temple was not decorated until the time of Augustus, the rooms show both pictorial and literary dedications by Ptolemy II to Isis. They are composed as if from the mouth of the king and honour Isis in a traditionally Egyptian manner. Accompanying the texts are various relief decorations, which again demonstrate the king's reverence to Isis and other gods. Around the base of the sanctuary in the innermost rooms, fertility gods are shown receiving Philadelphos; the higher registers throughout the temple emphasise the ruler's relationship with Isis, the divine protectress and mother of Horus. Arsinoe II also appears on five occasions with the goddess, thus emphasising her role as a goddess. In rooms I, VII and X of the temple, the queen adopts the same pose as Isis, distinguished only by her headdress. Her presence suggests that the priests of Philae accepted the worship of the queen even during the immediate period following her death and deification. Although there is no mention of Arsinoe in the hymns, which are reserved for Isis to whom the temple is dedicated, the queen appears on one occasion alone, in room V. Here Ptolemy offers a jar to his wife, who stands with a sceptre and ankh in hand, leaving no question of her divine status. The prominent use of Arsinoe's image in a native temple was a new phenomenon. It seems to have served two main purposes: firstly, it promoted the royal cult which stretched from Alexandria down to Philae; secondly, the association of the queen with Isis (who appears with her brother/consort Osiris) created an ideological and visual link to the sibling marriage of Ptolemy II and Arsinoe II.

Ptolemy II also added substantially to temples in the southern enclosure at Karnak, making architectural contributions to the gods Khonsu, who was one of the Theban triad; Mut, who was wife of Amun, and Apet, who was mother of Osiris. The Thebaid was an obvious target for royal patronage, since the priests of Amun who lived in the region were particularly powerful on account of their economic prosperity and also the geographical distance from the rulers in Alexandria. Amun was also important to the royal house because he was not only the personal deity of the king but had a close association with Alexander the Great, who was declared his son at Siwa. Ptolemy II also financed the building of a stone wall to enclose the temple of Amun at Hibis in Kharga Oasis. The original building dated from the 26th Dynasty and had been added to by the Persian ruler Darius I. Philadelphos surrounded the entire complex with a sandstone wall, decorated with traditional cavetto cornice. The motive for the ruler's patronage at the site was geographically, and perhaps also politically, removed from the main body of the sanctuaries along the Nile valley, and demonstrates an awareness of earlier dynasties which goes beyond the bounds of duty. Koptos, which marks the boundaries between Middle and Upper Egypt also received considerable attention during the reign of Ptolemy II, not least of all because his first wife was exiled there. The city was the capital of the fifth nome (or administrative centre) of Egypt, and during the Late Period the main sanctuary of the god Min also became important for the worship of Isis and Horus. Ptolemy II built the middle temple at the site, close to earlier structures that dated to the 28th Dynasty. There was also a temple to Min and Isis, which was dedicated by one of the ruler's officials named Sennu. The temple remained undecorated, which would imply that the ruling house felt no obligation to complete a project which, on the face of it, was on their behalf.

Ptolemy III continued his father's patronage of sites in Upper Egypt by completing a large gateway that was begun by Ptolemy II at Karnak. The ruler also targeted prominent areas of the complex in order to promote his dynasty. Propylons were a relatively economic way of self-advertisement; their size and position ensured immediate recognition and their use at Karnak, particularly by Ptolemy III Euergetes I, shows a political rather than religious motive for construction. This practice can be seen clearly in the building of a second gateway at the end of a processional walkway, lined by sphinxes, which leads from Karnak to Luxor. In the northern section of the site, Ptolemy III began another gateway that was close to the temple of the war god Montu, although this was completed by his son Ptolemy IV, and so bears his successor's personal decoration on the reliefs. Close to the gate, Ptolemy III made an addition to the temple of Ptah. The main chapel is reached through six gateways, the closest to the temple being part of the original building of Thutmose III, which was restored by Ptolemy III, probably when he commissioned what is now gate number five. Ptolemy III also left his cartouche on the temple of Amun. This can be found on the west face of the second pylon which was erected by Seti I, a 19th Dynasty ruler, and is further demonstration of a need to assert his presence at the site.

Further down the Nile Valley, Ptolemy III began the temple of Horus at Edfu in 237 BC on a site where there had previously been a shrine to the god, which went back to the 3rd Dynasty. The building itself was not dedicated until 42 BC during the reign of Cleopatra VII, the last Ptolemaic ruler. The temple is one of the best preserved in the pharaonic style and although none of the decorations shows the rulers who conceived or dedicated it, the reliefs offer an interesting insight to the relationship between king and priests. Horus was the falcon-headed son of Isis and Osiris and the pharaoh was traditionally seen to be the living embodiment of the god. Ptolemy III's extensive programme in honour of the god might also reflect his close association with the divine family, which had begun under his predecessor.

The building is a classic example of Ptolemaic temple design, and is all the more impressive today on account of its excellent state of preservation. The entrance is through the pylon, traditionally decorated with the king smiting his enemies, striding forward in a position and size that was symbolic of power. Directly behind the pylon is the Great court where members of the public were permitted to enter to either consult the god or attend festivals. Further back are the densely columned hypostyle halls, symbolic of the marshes from which the primeval mound of civilisation rose. In the second hall a series of reliefs shows Ptolemy IV laying the foundation plaques in the traditional Egyptian manner. There are seventeen plaques in total and the accompanying text describes the ruler placing the gold tablets at the corners of the building. This particular scene is not only of interest for its ritual subject matter but also because it shows how the later rulers were keen to take advantage of their ancestors' unfinished projects, without any apparent need to recognise their work. The various rooms behind the two halls, including the main sanctuary, show that the native religion continued its traditions unheeded by the advent of Macedonian rule. The ceremonial barque, which has been reconstructed from the Ptolemaic remains, was used for Horus's journey to neighbouring temples and confirms that Egyptian religious practices were maintained. On the walls of the ambulatory (a sort of corridor) on the north side of the temple, the god is shown in his role as protector of Egypt defeating his brother Seth (in the form of a hippopotamus) who, by this period in the Nile Valley, represented evil and chaos.

Since the pharaoh represented the living Horus, these texts would appear to honour the ruling house. However, in a paper written in 1971, Fairman criticised this interpretation and suggested that the local priests saw Ptolemy not as Horus but as Seth, the foreigner and the enemy. He referred to the rebellions and anti-Ptolemaic Egyptian literature that occurred later in the dynasty to support his argument. The so-called 'oracle of the potter' predicted that the native pharaohs (Senusret III, Ramesses II or Nectanebo II) would return and save Egypt from foreign rule. Interestingly, many of the cartouches were left blank or only partially complete. This may have been due to the lack of certainty in the reign of Ptolemy VIII and continuing during the reigns of his sons Ptolemies IX and X over who was ruling Egypt – a situation that was the result of dynastic rivalry culminating in rulers being exiled abroad. Many scholars have criticised Fairman's interpretation of the Edfu reliefs and it is of further interest to note that during native rebellions in Upper Egypt the temples and priests often found themselves on the receiving end of abuse by the rebels on account of their relationship with the royal house. It is important to note that the Ptolemaic rulers gave the priests considerable concessions and often used monies from taxation to fund priesthoods, often related to the royal cults. Furthermore, without a pharaoh, the traditional unification of Upper and Lower Egypt, which was performed at his coronation, could not have taken place, thus allowing chaos to rule. For this reason a foreign pharaoh would have seemed preferable to none at all, and the inscriptions in the various chapels attest that the rituals between priest and god followed the traditions of earlier periods. The foundation of an entirely new project by Ptolemy III, where noticeable additions sufficed, might imply a genuine religious or political commitment on his behalf.

Ptolemy III also continued his father's patronage of Isis in Upper Egypt. In the modern town of Aswan, east of the river

Nile and opposite Elephantine Island stands an unfinished temple to the goddess. The main doorway reveals the only evidence of Ptolemy III's contribution to the building; the scenes here show the king offering to the Theban triad Amun, Mut and Khonsu. On the lintel the ruler and his wife, Berenike II, offer to the gods but do not themselves receive honours. Their status is not therefore divine in the sense that they are worshipped as individuals. The temple interior remains undecorated and the plan is very simple, consisting of a small main hall with three adjoining chapels.

The temples and areas patronised by the first three rulers laid the foundations for their successors, sometimes quite literally on which to build, and their commitment to the native Egyptian traditions illustrates a certain commitment to their new country. The rulers didn't simply attempt to Hellenise Egypt but decided rather to acknowledge their new culture and promote it to the Greek communities in their new capital.

Perversely, the most prolific period of temple building during Ptolemaic rule occurred during the rather troubled reign of Ptolemy VIII Euergetes II. Not only did the ruler patronise large-scale projects, but he also completed sites that were linked to the 30th Dynasty and had remained incomplete for a century or more, often in outposts such as Hibis in Kharga Oasis. Scholars have long argued over the identity of key portrait types, being split between the 30th Dynasty and Ptolemies VIII, IX and X. This delayed interest in sites where earlier Egyptian sculptors had worked may well explain this, at first, incongruous confusion, 200 years apart.

Ptolemy VIII built a birth house at Philae and completed the decoration of other parts of the temple, where, as noted, there were structures dating to the reigns of Ptolemy II and the 30th Dynasty. At Koptos – which had received a new enclosure wall during the reign of Nectanebo I and a new temple under Ptolemy II – Ptolemy VIII built a monumental gateway. His keenness to be associated with the 30th Dynasty and early Ptolemaic building works is further illustrated by the completion of the projects at Karnak, begun by his ancestors. Here, the ruler finished the temple of Opet, which had also involved Ptolemy III. Arnold has argued that this particular building may have been seen as the birth house of the god Khonsu; in Egyptian mythology Amun was believed to have died in the form of Osiris and to have entered the body of the goddess Nut-Opet, to be reborn as Khonsu. The ruler also dedicated birth houses at Edfu and Kom Ombo, and at Philae an addition was made to the existing temple, which required the original north wall to be removed and the northern portico to be resited. Such works illustrate more than simple completion projects and more a desire to expand or rebuild. A birth house was also built on Elephantine Island, at Aswan. At the temple of Monthu at Medamoud the extent of the somewhat destructive nature of the 'developments' that occurred during the reign of Ptolemy VIII become apparent. Here, the builders re-used blocks from earlier buildings dating to the Late period and the early Ptolemaic period. Arnold suggests that the gates and chapels to which this material belonged were probably sacrificed as part of the second-century BC expansion. Politically inspired repairs were also undertaken at this site during the reign of Ptolemy VIII. A small chapel – perhaps a birth house dating to the reign of Ptolemy III that had been damaged in the native rebellions of 207/6 BC during the reign of Ptolemy IV – was rebuilt, but, as Arnold notes, the foundations and parts of the masonry, some of which dated to the Middle and New Kingdoms, were maintained, resulting in a chronological hybrid of styles. Although it is difficult to establish whether such building projects were undertaken solely on account of royal policy, completion of earlier projects must have linked the rulers to their predecessors. In all, Ptolemy VIII was involved in ten building projects, some of which were continued by his two feuding sons. The only other ruler to compete with Ptolemy VIII's enthusiasm for patronising Egyptian temples was Ptolemy XII, a ruler who also, it could be said, needed the support of the Egyptian priesthood because of his unpopularity among the Alexandrians, which at times led to both rulers being exiled from Egypt.

Ptolemy XII was nicknamed *Auletes* (the flute-player) by the Alexandrians, but he was also known as *nothos* (the bastard). The former name probably stems from his affiliation to Dionysos, the Greek god of wine; the latter because he was illegitimate and there is some doubt about the identity of his mother. It is this unknown aspect that has led to the suggestion that Cleopatra VII, his daughter, may have been at least part Nubian and so black. The reign was somewhat troubled, although compared to the problems that immediately preceded the coronation of Ptolemy XII, his reign can be seen as one of the high points of the later Ptolemaic period. Temple projects during this period included some that had been started by his immediate predecessors, Ptolemies IX and X (the reign of Ptolemy XI being of little significance as it lasted only a matter of weeks). It is possible that royal finances simply survived the changes in regime, but the fact that the rulers continued to support native Egyptian temples is instructive and illustrates a willingness to maintain good relations with the priests who formed the Egyptian élite.

Ptolemy XII was in part responsible for some of Egypt's most visited temples. He began the replacement of a 30th Dynasty temple of Hathor at Denderah in 54 BC, and this project continued through the reigns of his children and into the Roman period; it was completed in 20 BC, some 10 years after the death of Cleopatra VII. It is perhaps best known for the offering scene on the south wall (Figure 3) which shows Cleopatra and her son Caesarion. Ptolemy XII (*Auletes*) also made additions to the temple at Koptos in the form of a gate within the great enclosure, which dates to the 30th Dynasty. He also continued the work of Ptolemy VIII at Edfu, and the courtyard and pylon of the temple were completed in 70 BC and it is in fact his image in the smiting scene that decorates the front of the temple. At Karnak, the gateway leading to the temple of Ptah was added and at nearby Deir el-Medina (perhaps better known as the workman's village of the New Kingdom) the ruler surrounded the temple of Hathor with an enclosure wall. Other notable projects included the temple of Kom Ombo, where a new monumental gateway was built, and

Philae, where the ruler appears on the walls' first pylon and courtyard, by means of completing an earlier Ptolemaic project.

This brief survey of temples is not exhaustive, but it is enough to illustrate the extent of the commitment by the Ptolemaic royal house to the Egyptian tradition. The involvement of individual queens will be considered further in Chapter 5, but the rulers' dedications help to explain the relationship between the kings as high priests and their representatives in the form of priests. Egyptian temples replicated, on an enormous scale, the early Ptolemaic rulers' promotion of Greek culture at the Mouseion in Alexandria.

Alexandria

In addition to acting as a role model for the Ptolemaic pharaohs, Alexander the Great also gave credibility to what would become the new capital, by selecting the site and confirming its status by consulting the same Siwan oracle that declared him to be a living god. The ruler's stay in Egypt was too short to allow for anything more than foundations to be planned and much of the development of the city was undertaken by Ptolemies I, II and III, with subsequent additions made to the palaces by each ruler. Following his conquest of Egypt in 332 BC, Alexander did not return and died nine years later in 323 BC. The Ptolemaic rulers then had a blessed but blank canvas on which to build their city and the perfect role model on which they could mould their own presentation. This relationship was cemented by the hi-jacking of Alexander's funeral cortege on its route from Babylon to Macedonia. The body was taken firstly to Memphis, which lies close to modern Cairo, and then to Alexandria to be interred in a mausoleum, which also became the focal point of the dynastic cults of Alexander and the Ptolemies.

The royal cults, which will be discussed in greater detail in Chapter 6 with respect to the role played by the Ptolemaic queens, infiltrated not only Egyptian temples as already seen, but were prominent in the capital. Many of the temples were related to ruler worship, or as noted in the case of Sarapis, the rulers' association with the gods. Individual rulers, such as Arsinoe, were awarded their own temples – this particular example, according to Pliny, complete with a floating statue, supported by a magnetic force. Later, during the reign of Cleopatra VII, a temple was begun for the deified Julius Caesar, most probably in order to stress the status of her son, Caesarion. The tomb of Alexander and the temples to rulers were all situated close to the royal palaces, which occupied the coastal region, now under water. It was also within this region that the famous Mouseion and library of the Ptolemies were located, no doubt to enable the rulers to keep a close watch on their scholars' activities. The institution functioned as a sort of élite university and became a magnet for philosophers, poets and writers from throughout the Greek world.

Strabo, visiting Alexandria in the late first century BC, described the Mouseion as a place of shaded walkways and arcades with recesses and seats; a place where men could work uninhibited by outside worries. The reality, however, was a tightly controlled institution where scholars quarrelled among themselves and members were encouraged to promote their patrons. One particular scholar who foolishly criticised the sibling marriage of Ptolemy II and Arsinoe II was murdered.

Art and artistic innovation ought to have mirrored the literary achievements of the Mouseion, for both were dependent on royal patronage and both could promote the royal family. By the reign of Ptolemy VIII, however the Alexandrian wits had begun to mock their rulers, naming this particular ruler, whose cult name was Euergetes II, *Physon* or Fatty. His successors followed similar fates, Ptolemy IX being named Chickpea, although the reasons for this particular name are unclear. Images of the rulers would have been placed within the palaces, public areas and sanctuaries – as illustrated by a number of representations in both Greek and Egyptian styles of Ptolemaic queens – and each will be discussed in some detail in Chapters 4, 5 and 6. One particular example (illustrated in Figure 6) was found within the royal palaces and appears to be unfinished; suggesting that work-shops were housed close to their patrons. We know from models that were found at Memphis that the male royal image was dis-seminated from probably central workshops to the provinces, and the surviving representations of queens support this hypoth-esis with their recognisable portrait types for each queen. Their Egyptian-style images, however, seem to have copied the features of the ruler and transposed them, sometimes with dramatic result, as illustrated in Figure 25 (see p. 139).

There has been little in terms of archaeological evidence to support Alexandria's claim to being the leading artistic centre in Ptolemaic Egypt. Evidence from Memphis suggests that there was at least local production at this particular site of both Greek and Egyptian materials, including pottery, faience objects and vessels, royal sculpture, bronze figurines and terracotta figurine production. In other words, the artists at Memphis catered for their immediate audience, and it is likely that other areas did the same. Artists and artisans would base themselves where there was an immediate audience, and sanctuaries such as Memphis pro-vided the perfect environment for the production of objects that would have acted as either votives or souvenirs for the many visi-tors as well as residents of the city. It is impossible to know if an Alexandrian equivalent to the Memphis workshops existed, because much of the ancient city remains under modern dwellings and has not been systematically excavated. There are several indications that goods, such as Greek funerary hydriai (water jugs), were imported from Crete and, it is thought, copied locally. Certainly with the festivals, royal cult centre, palaces, harbours and cemeteries of Alexandria had all of the ingredients to warrant the production of material culture, but if simple vases were being imported from Crete then one has to question this particular claim to fame.

The past five years of archaeological investigations in the area around fort Quait Bey (which was traditionally believed to have housed the famous lighthouse), the cemetery of Gabbari and, in terms of the city's topography, the mapping of the original harbours, have revealed a number of surprises. Because of the Mouseion and libraries, which were predominantly concerned with Greek culture, scholars have for many years treated Alexandria as a city 'ad Aegyptum'; a Greek *polis* (city) attached to Egypt and a promoter of classical rather than Egyptian culture. Until recently, the city provided an exotic haven for the classical scholars, who felt secure in the knowledge that they were dealing with a wholly Greek institution. What many early archaeologists and art historians failed to recognise, however, were the many Egyptian features that made up Ptolemaic Alexandria. Until recently little attention has been paid to Egyptian monuments within the city, but the mapping of find-spots for this material reveals a carefully planned presentation of the Egyptian face of the Ptolemaic royal family that leaves no doubt about where their allegiances lay.

In 1993 Tkaczow produced an archaeological map of Alexandria, pinpointing known find-spots for material within the Greco-Roman Museum. By using this, in conjunction with individual reports for single objects that have been found within the city over the last hundred years, it is possible to see that key areas were targeted for the promotion of Egyptian culture in the third century BC, and that by the second century BC, the city had adopted a strong native presence. Strabo noted that by the first century BC the city was divided into 'quarters' according to ethnic groups, but the archaeological record has shown that irrespective of an individual's ancestral origins all were exposed to Egyptian culture. As already mentioned, the cult of Sarapis was used by the early Ptolemies to introduce traditional Egyptian deities to the Greeks in the city; the placing of the temple to this ambassador was in the oldest part of Alexandria, which, before Alexander, had been the city of Rhakotis. At this sanctuary was a small temple to the goddess Isis, who became arguably one of the most important envoys for Egyptian religion in both the Greek and Roman worlds. Then, as noted, the early rulers commissioned two colossal sphinxes in the Egyptian style to remind visitors of the principal god's origins as well as their adoptive culture.

One area where Greek culture seems to have dominated is in the burial practices of Alexandrians. Those sites that have been excavated have revealed burials and material culture that accords with Greek traditions. Traditional Egyptian materials, such as faience, are found but they are in forms that are inspired by the classical world, such as the wine jugs with images of Ptolemaic queens pouring a libation at an altar, as illustrated in Figure 5. Elsewhere, moulded vessels in forms found outside Egypt in other Hellenistic cities were also made of faience. Such objects were placed in graves or loculi (rock cut tombs) with the deceased's ashes held in one of the Cretan hydriai, often with the name of the deceased inscribed on the shoulder of the vessel. However, the discovery in August 2002 of what from initial reports appears to be an élite Egyptian dating to the pre-Ptolemaic period, may change our perceptions of this particular aspect of the city.

The many processions and festivals that took place in the city also appear, from their descriptions by Greek authors, to have been concerned with Greek gods and, of course, the newly deified rulers themselves. The Pompe of Ptolemy Philadelphos was described in Athenodoros' *Athenaeus Deipnosophistai* and was by all accounts an elaborate and extravagant affair that involved a series of processions with a common link of copious amounts of wine for all of those who took part. Mechanical statues poured wine to the spectators; mock caverns, spewing forth yet more wine – and a large part of the proceedings dedicated to who else but the god of wine, Dionysos, with whom many of the Ptolemies felt a close personal affiliation – set the scene for what must have been an amazing sight for those who could remain upright for the entire occasion. Once again, many early commentators, who were better versed in the classical tradition, failed to see the overt Egyptian overtones of such events. The gods may have been Greek, but the concept must have been influenced by the native Egyptian divine processions. It is against this bicultural and bilingual backdrop that we must view Ptolemaic Egypt, and by its very nature the adjective Ptolemaic has its own quite distinctive character.

Memphis, the second city

Memphis was the main religious centre for Middle Egypt (an artificial boundary which runs from the city southwards to Lycopolis, modern Assyut). During the early Ptolemaic period Middle Egypt became a settlement zone, particularly around the Faiyum, where many Macedonian and other immigrant soldiers made their homes alongside native Egyptians. This phenomenon has been well documented in the papyri, which are a valuable source of information on population origin and Ptolemaic administration, both of which have been the subject of several studies and monographs.

Memphis represented an important religious centre for the region. The city traditionally dates back to the 1st Dynasty (3000–2890 BC) and enjoyed the position of capital of Egypt into the Old Kingdom (2686–2125 BC). It was later made capital under Cleomenes, the financial manager and administration chief of Alexander the Great, who unofficially declared himself *satrap* (governor) following the ruler's death. By the time of the Ptolemaic period Memphis was in many respects a divided city; in the west, close to the desert edge at Saqqara, were the sacred animal cemeteries, and to the east was the valley, a desert region where the palaces, temples and homes to a mixed population were situated. The city was initially home to the Ptolemaic rulers, and again became the royal residence under Ptolemy V. It was also the place where the Ptolemaic rulers were crowned pharaoh. The earliest recorded example of this dates to the reign of Ptolemy V, but given the interest in their role as pharaoh from the start of the dynasty, many scholars believe that earlier rulers were also crowned according to the Egyptian tradition. Memphis was also the place of celebration for Ptolemy IX's sed (30 year jubilee) festival in 88 BC, even though the ruler was exiled for some of this period, during which time his brother ruled Egypt.

The rulers were able to show their support for the native Egyptian religion early in the dynasty. Not long after Ptolemy I came to power, one of the Apis bulls died and the ruler offered a loan to pay for its burial. The burial and associated ceremonies presented a costly affair, and a duty that fell upon the royal house to fulfil. Strabo's description of the parading of the Apis bull is a delightful insight into tourism at the site. We are told that the bull was housed within a stall, and that at designated hours the priests would parade the animal in front of an appreciative crowd. It is probable that the many terracotta examples of bulls' heads found at the site were bought by devotees of the cult and either dedicated there, or perhaps taken home as a souvenir. The bulls bred at the site, but the offspring of the 'reigning' bull would not necessarily be its successor; the bulls were chosen for their specific markings and, following the death of the primary bull, a nation-wide search ensued. Once found the new bull, and often its immediate 'family' were transferred to Memphis, where it would live out its days in relative peace and security. It is around the Saqqara section of the city, where the bulls were buried, that the majority of the archaeological evidence for royal patronage has been found. A hieroglyphic cartouche of Ptolemy I's name was found on the eastern headland, but there are no further remains of the building to which it belonged. A second cartouche bearing the hieroglyphic name of Ptolemy II was also retrieved from the site, carved into a cavetto cornice, which Thompson suggests perhaps belonged to the major building works of 253 to 248 BC, the costs of which are listed in an inscription. This programme included a new building for the Apis bull from the cow Ta-Renenutet, and a shrine for the cow goddess Hathor. The same builder completed not only the temple to the cat goddess Bastet, which housed the priests, but also two or three other structures, including temples to Horus, Thoth and Nekhthoreb the falcon god.

Close to the temple of Bastet was the temple of Anubis, the chthonic god of mummification. Like the complex above, the sanctuary had occupied the site prior to the Ptolemaic period and no further additions were made until the time of Ptolemy V. However, the temple was joined to a major new sanctuary that was funded by either Ptolemy I or II. This was the Sarapieion, which Fraser believes was built on the site of an already established cult to the god Osiris-Apis shortly after its Alexandrian sister. The sanctuary was appropriately connected to the temple of Anubis by an avenue of Egyptian sphinxes, echoing the traditional Egyptian practice. However, much of the imagery was Greek and the rulers took the opportunity to assert their Greek cultural heritage at the site in the form of a hemicycle of Greek philosophers and poets.

The statues were discovered by Auguste Mariette in 1853 during an attempt to locate the burial chambers for the Apis bulls. The Greek sculptures seem to have been a frustration to Mariette as he gradually worked his way up the dromos in hope of locating the chambers that housed the dead Apis bulls. Mariette did, however, make detailed sketches of the pieces and the dromos, but it was not until a year after his death in 1882 that his notes were published by his successor Gaston Maspero. Ulrich Wilcken then wrote a second very detailed publication in 1917, although this concentrates on the sculpture from the dromos. In 1950 another French team returned to the site, under the direction of Jean-Philippe Lauer and Charles Picard. Their publication was heavily influenced by Mariette's original work, and they agree with his original interpretation and identification of the statues.

The hemicycle is closer to the temple of Nectanebo (in honour of an unknown deity) than to the Sarapieion and, contrary to popular belief, the group bears no reference to the Sarapis, except for the possible assimilation of Dionysos to Sarapis, since the main group is accompanied by a Dionysiac procession. The hemicycle would have been reached via an avenue of 30th Dynasty sphinxes but effectively blocks the earlier sculptural decoration from outside the temple of Nectanebo; the exedra is placed in the most prominent position, at the end of the 30th Dynasty dromos, at the turning point before the visitors walk up the main complex and burial chambers. The visitors would have proceeded towards the Sarapieion, past the temple of Nectanebo and have seen the Ptolemaic group immediately upon turning right into the main dromos. Past the hemicycle a Dionysiac procession would have led the visitors further, the group itself appearing to be heading towards the main temple area. Then, past several smaller shrines, the visitors would have walked on a pathway to the temple complex. Thus, both the hemicycle and the procession played an integral role in the approach to the Sarapieion and other temples; one greeted the visitors, the other directed the way to the gods, and perhaps offered a hint of one of the festivals to be attended, for Dionysos fulfilled a Bacchic rather than a chthonic role. The identity of the members of the main group is not known and has been exacerbated by their poor state of preservation. It is possible, however, that it included men such as Homer, Pythagoras, Plato, Herodotus, Solon, Pindar, Thales and Socrates; in other words, those who had a connection with Egypt.

The date of the dedication of this group has also been much debated, although scholars generally place it within the early Ptolemaic period. There is one extremely fragmentary portrait of a ruler, which is similar to that of Ptolemy IV. The fact that the statues are purely Greek in style would also suggest that they were no later than the end of his reign; from the reign of Ptolemy V there is a growing trend in Egypt for the rulers to draw on both Greek and Egyptian traditions in sculpture, particularly at Egyptian sanctuaries. At Memphis and at the Sarapieion in Alexandria the parallel dedications respect the individual traditions. This fact would suggest that the date of the monument at Memphis falls within the reigns of the first four rulers.

There are two further reasons to link Ptolemy IV Philopator with the dedication. Firstly, there is the strong Dionysiac theme: although many of the Ptolemaic rulers associated themselves with Dionysos, it was Ptolemy IV who had a particular connection with the god, an association that was matched only by that of Ptolemy XII, who took the title Neos Dionysos. Secondly, it may even be possible to link the monument to a specific year and event. In 217 BC Ptolemy IV was involved in a dispute with

Antiochus III over Coele-Syria. The decisive battle occurred at Raphia on 22 June and Ptolemy was victorious. The battle was significant in more ways than one, since it was the first time that a Ptolemy had used large numbers of native Egyptian soldiers to fight on his behalf. In November of 217 BC there was a priestly synod at Memphis, and the king's achievements were celebrated on the Raphia stela. At the top of the text is a traditional scene showing Ptolemy IV on horseback, accompanied by his wife, Arsinoe, standing before the Egyptian gods. What is interesting is that Ptolemy wears a Macedonian battle-dress and not the traditional Egyptian kilt. In many ways this representation parallels the presence of the Greek statues at the Memphis Sarapieion; it was also to Memphis that Ptolemy IV returned following this campaign.

The Apis bull and its Greek offspring, Sarapis, were not the only gods to call Memphis their home. As mentioned, the bull was believed to be the living representative of Ptah, the god of craftsmen, among other things. There was a sizeable temple dedicated to Ptah along with temples to the goddesses Hathor, Aphrodite and Astarte; all three being equivalents in Egyptian, Greek and Near Eastern cultures. Also close to this religious centre were the embalming houses for the Apis bulls, where a colossal stone table accommodated the bulls during their mummification. Even today, with the temples in ruins and divided by vegetation – and in the case of the embalming house, a modern road – it is easy to imagine what must have once provided a buzzing atmosphere of pilgrimage, festivals and the activities associated with the day-to-day running of the temples. The priests here were Egyptians and must have provided the Ptolemies with their all-important allies within this élite social group. More importantly, it was in the Ptah temple where the rulers were crowned, which elevated the status of the priests of Ptah. The bonding of this relationship can be seen clearly in the interaction between ruler and what was effectively Ptolemaic Egypt's second city. There are accounts of rulers visiting the site in person, and as Thompson notes, such visits increased during the second century BC. There is also considerable archaeological evidence for the patronage of the temples and gods of Memphis by the early Ptolemies. In addition to making Arsinoe II a temple sharing the goddess of Ptah, Ptolemy II dedicated an individual temple to his sister and wife, following her death. It is believed to have been located close to the Ptah temple and the royal palaces.

It was around the Ptah temple, perhaps not coincidentally, that the main production centre appears to have been focused. Terracotta figurines, faience vessels and figurines, and bronze statuettes were all manufactured on site, presumably to satiate the demand of pilgrims wishing to pay for and leave a dedication to a god. The types of objects found show a wide range of forms and types, including both Greek and Egyptian figures. The terracottas also illustrate an attempt by Egyptian artists to produce terracottas that would appeal to Greek worshippers, made according to their own traditions but with Greek iconography. There is no such reciprocal copying by Greek artists, however, which is a common observation when considering Greek material culture in Egypt both pre- and post-Ptolemaic occupation. Many were excavated by Sir William Mathew Flinders Petrie, with the largest collection now housed in the Petrie Museum of Egyptian Archaeology, London. The terracottas were first published by Petrie in his excavation reports of Memphis, volumes I, II and III; in the accompanying discussion he writes '... the discovery of the portraits of the foreigners was not even thought of; and only gradually was it realised that we had before us the figures of more than a dozen different races' (Petrie, *Memphis* I, 1909: 15). Petrie classified the terracotta heads under the categories of Greek, Egyptian, Persian, Sumerian, Semitic Babylonian, Indian (of which there are Tibetan and Aryan Punjabi types), Scythian and Roman, adding the following in *Memphis*, volume II: Iberian, Carian, Hebrew, Kurd, Ionian Greek and Mesopotamian. His classifications have recently been challenged, and many of the terracottas that are distinctive on account of the bald, misshapen heads can be identified as representations of Egyptian priests, who were required to shave their hair before an offering to the god. Even though the figures do not seem to represent the various races to whom they were attributed, the presence of Persian, Greek and Egyptian forms suggests that artists were flexible and able to produce whatever forms of representation the general public required. It is somewhat ironic that the artists and artisans of a form of art now considered to be one of the most rigid in terms of its style were able to turn their talents to whatever the buyers demanded.

Also within this area, there was a large temple of an earlier Egyptian ruler named Merenptah who ruled Egypt from 1213 to 1203 BC. Petrie believed that the foreign quarter of Memphis was centred around this area, and early Greek pottery was found at the site. The distribution of finds by the late Ptolemaic period, however, suggests that Greeks and Egyptians lived and worshipped side by side. When the first century BC geographer, Strabo (*Geographies* 17.1.32), visited Memphis he commented that: 'The city is both large and populous, it ranks second after Alexandria and its population is a mixed one.' Even before the Ptolemaic conquest, Memphis had enjoyed a multi-cultural society. There is considerable evidence of the settlement of Carians (from the south-west of modern Turkey), and that Persian rulers had built their palace at the site of a raised mound, close to the main temple complexes. Today very little remains, but the size of the column capitals suggests that the structure was of a considerable size and splendour. Thompson listed the evidence for other groups of settlers in the city, which included Ionian Greeks, Carians from the sixth century BC, mainland Greeks, Macedonian Greeks, Phoenicians, Jews and other Semitic settlers prior to Alexander's conquest of Egypt in 332 BC, and Idumaeans (from southern Judaea).

Memphis is often eclipsed by Alexandria, but the archaeological and textual evidence from the site surpasses that from Alexandria in many respects. This observation is clearly not only coincidence, and it is clear that the Ptolemies realised the potential of this established but cosmopolitan Egyptian centre.

Royal 'art'

The concept of 'art' is not always appropriate or accurate in relation to ancient cultures and yet in Ptolemaic Egypt it unashamedly flourished. The Ptolemies, like other Hellenistic dynasts, used art in its most extreme form as a means of propaganda and at the very least as a means of promoting themselves and their dynasty. Images of the rulers are one way in which art served a purpose that was more than decorative; but closely linked to this function, and indeed probably the greatest impetus for artistic representation, was religion. Of course religion and politics were never far apart, and it is the images of the Ptolemaic royal women that in many respects allow us the closest insight into the development of their roles in Egypt and the most immediately identifiable link with the country's past. From colossal sculpture to coin portrait, artistic representation was the easiest means of reaching the illiterate masses; people learnt to interpret these images and so, when the appropriate iconography was used, the king and queen were recognised by all.

One of the most intriguing features of Ptolemaic material culture is the lack of synthesis of the two dominant styles. The papyri indicate that there were cross-cultural marriages and that some individuals took both Greek and Egyptian names depending on whether they were in an official or a domestic situation, but nowhere is this replicated in objects of daily use or in official 'art'. What this phenomenon illustrates is the ability of both Greek and Egyptian artists to adopt, and then appropriately adapt, features or concepts from an alien culture. Although some early publications refer to the so-called mixed-style of art, this phenomenon is actually a rather complex borrowing of key features from the Greek culture by Egyptian artists. This effectively makes the male statues bilingual because the subject appears as pharaoh with the appropriate attributes, but reveals a Greek portrait comparable to that circulated on the coinage and known to the communities where Greek-style statuary was displayed.

The Egyptian-style male royal representations show a clear two-phase development, which is, in some respects, mirrored by the representations of the queens. Firstly, portrait features are adopted from the Greek repertoire. Some of the early examples, dating to the reigns of Ptolemy V and Ptolemy VI, are so well executed that the Egyptian artist has produced a higher quality rendering of the facial features and hair than the surviving Greek originals. So fine is the hair on one particular portrait of Ptolemy VI that it has been suggested that the sculptor was working from a bronze model rather than a stone Greek original. The inclusion of hair under the traditional Egyptian headdress is also a non-Egyptian feature; the headdress usually covers any hair on male royal portraits and so its appearance in the Ptolemaic period must have been in order to maintain the familiar Greek-style portrait of the rulers. Why did the Egyptian artists suddenly start to use Greek attributes on their sculpture? There are two possible explanations for this phenomenon, one of which is political. During the last years of the reign of Ptolemy IV, and also during the first part of the reign of his successor, Ptolemy V, rebel native pharaohs ruled in the south of Egypt. The earliest possible statue to show these features (although its identity is disputed) is a colossal granite representation of Ptolemy V, now in the Egyptian Museum Cairo, but said to have been found at Karnak. It is possible that the inclusion of Greek portrait features of this foreign pharaoh, the rightful king, were manufactured in order to distinguish the Ptolemies from their rivals in the south; the dedication of such a statue at Karnak can only have been a politically inspired move. Around the time of the appearance of these representations, sculptors' models cease to be produced and it is possible that Egyptian artists were forced to turn to Greek portraits for models.

These models come in two distinct forms: plaque relief representations and busts of varying sizes showing the face and sometimes headdress of the ruler. They occur in plaster and also in limestone. The former were probably used as part of the manufacturing process of carving a sculpture, where casts are taken before the final piece is executed. This allows the subject or artist to decide on the final form of 'portrait' before taking his chisel to the rather more costly stone. The purpose behind the plaques is not, however, as easily determined and some scholars believe them to be ex-votos or dedications on behalf of the royal cults rather than a relief equivalent of the bust representations. Indeed, some examples carry either Greek or demotic inscriptions, indicating that this was their purpose. The busts are, like early Ptolemaic Egyptian-style statues, remarkably like the images of the 30th Dynasty rulers and it is likely that this association was part of a deliberate policy by the rulers to link them to the last Egyptian dynasty, working very much in a similar way to their completion of temple building projects by this particular dynasty.

From the reign of Ptolemy VIII, however, we find an interesting development occurring, not only with regard to the reappearance of Egyptian sculptors' models, but also in the second phase of the development of the male royal image. This is the production of versions of Greek portraits. By version I mean that the portrait is modelled on a Greek portrait type but shows no Greek characteristics. This is clearly visible on the so-called *physcon* (pot-belly or fatty) portraits of Ptolemy VIII. On the Egyptian-style representations, a large bloated face appears but carved in such a manner that is typical of the slightly stylised Egyptian form. There are a handful of models from this period that suggests that artists were once again forced to produce their own versions of the royal portrait and so reverted to traditional means to execute this plan. Some of the versions have hair, others do not, and the result is a somewhat stylised portrait attached to a traditional statue of a striding king.

A certain amount of confusion is caused by the re-carving of earlier statues during this period of considerable unrest in Egypt. Certain characteristics are also passed on from one generation to another, most notably the hooked nose which first appears on the portraits of Ptolemy VIII and continues through to the reign of Cleopatra VII, and may well account for the queen's famous feature. This is a clever means of linking oneself with one's predecessors and is not necessarily indicative of true, life-like features. The so-called *physcon* portraits that occur during the reign of Ptolemies VIII, IX and X, however, may well have been true to life. We know from historical sources that all three rulers were hugely overweight and were in fact called *physcon* by the Alexandrians. Far from being ashamed of their size, the rulers appear to have been rather proud of their large proportions and Ptolemy VIII is said to have worn a diaphanous robe.

The early Greek portraits follow a similar pattern to their Egyptian counterparts before the merger of presentations. Ptolemies I and II opted for an idealised but kingly portrait type as illustrated by that on their coins, showing Alexander the Great at the same time, with divine attributes and heroic portrait features. During the reign of Ptolemy III, however, the ruler adopts known divine attributes on his coin portraits in order to associate himself with the gods Zeus, Poseidon and Helios. It is likely that his stone portraits showed the same links with Greek divinities and in many respects his move to so blatantly promote himself as a divine figure pushed the development of the Ptolemaic royal image forwards. His successors continued the tradition and there are silver coins showing either Ptolemy IV or V with the ivy crown of Dionysos.

It is tempting for the modern viewer to assume that the Greek-style portraits are closer than their Egyptian counterparts to the rulers' true appearances; however, this is unlikely to have been the case. Hellenistic Greek portraits present an idealised or heroic form of image and those that appear to be veristic or realistic are classified as psychological portrait types. In other words, the viewer sees the personality of the subject. The one exception to this general rule may well be the *physcon* portraits, simply because we know that the subjects were fat. In such cases, however, scholars have argued that what we see is the Hellenistic characteristic of *luxury*, promoting the idea that the subject can afford to be well rounded and indulge in hedonistic rather than practical pursuits.

So, image was as much about how a person wanted to be per-ceived as it was about how they might have looked, and the sim-ilarity between generations of rulers was often a simple means of promoting the 'rightful' successor. The fortunes of the Ptolemies are nowhere more apparent than on coinage. Firstly, as the for-tunes dwindle, the coinage is debased and so is less valuable. On a very simple level this can be seen by the cessation of gold coinage after the reign of Ptolemy VI and the fact that the por-traits of Ptolemies IX and X do not decorate the obverse of coins minted during their reign. Many rulers used the image of their founder Ptolemy I, and his portrait type remains standard throughout the dynasty's history. Queens also appeared on coinage, as will be seen in Chapters 4 and 6 below. For art his-torians, these inscribed and identifiable images have provided a basis on which to identify non-inscribed portraits, including those made in stone. While this is a helpful tool, it should be used with caution simply because of the scale of the coins and their variety of forms, depending on the mint.

Sealings (clay stamp impressions) are also helpful particularly for those rulers who do not appear on coins, namely Ptolemies IX and X. The two brothers shared similar portrait traits but the problem of identification is exacerbated by the fact that Ptolemy IX was exiled part way through his reign and his brother took control of Egypt. Their images are probably as far from idealised as it is possible to be: large hooked noses, jowls and inflated faces. It was unfortunate that their queens emulated their portrait type.

The rulers also patronised art such as painting. Their presence in the artistic economy, therefore, was not only felt through the promotion of their image or of the many building projects they sponsored, they were also essentially the private collectors of their day. Just as their officials confiscated any written work that happened to dock in the harbour (to be copied for the original owners while the original documents were placed in the library) – and in the same way that Ptolemy II collected exotic animals in his private zoo – paintings and mosaic within the palaces must have been of an extremely high standard. A mosaic excavated at the new Alexandrian library site, which in Ptolemaic times would have been the royal palaces, shows a rather forlorn dog who has just knocked over a jug; not only does this piece show the quality of craftsmanship available at the time (the tesserae blocks are so small that they are only just visible) but it also demonstrates the more human side of Ptolemaic art and one with which we can easily identify today. Other recorded examples of art were simply bizarre. In the temple of Homer built by Ptolemy IV in Alexandria, there was according to literary sources a painting showing the divine poet Homer vomiting, and surrounding him were other philosophers and poets symbolically eating the vomit from the master's mouth.

Ptolemaic women

The 1998 sourcebook of *Women and Society in Greek and Roman Egypt* offers an insight into women in Egypt during the Ptolemaic period through the papyrological record. Petitions, letters and legal documents allow the modern viewer unique access to everyday life and its problems in Egypt at this time. The papyri offer a glimpse of aspects of everyday life from property deals and disputes, marriage and divorce settlements, to the more personal complaints about neighbours and, in one instance, an incompetent bath attendant who scalded a woman, to the letters from wives to their husbands, who, attracted to the bright lights of Alexandria, are behind in their maintenance payments. Some of the letters or petitions were written by women, illustrating some literacy among them. In other instances documents state that the author was not the writer, and either professional scribal services or simply those of a family member or friend were employed to write on the individual's behalf.

It is possible that with regards to the rights to own property, the Ptolemaic queens set a precedent. We know from the textual records that Princess Berenike, daughter of Ptolemy III and Berenike II, owned a vineyard; that Cleopatra II owned considerable holdings in her own name, and a barge. Obviously, such material wealth was limited to the élite classes, but there is evidence for non-royal women with similar holdings at this time. Such powers were not normal in the Greek world, and the Macedonian women who settled in Egypt enjoyed a degree of emancipation, in legal terms at least. The papyri show that women certainly did not suffer injustices in silence, often playing on their vulnerability when petitioning the king. One particular example, written by a woman named Asia, dating to 28 January 222 BC, and included in Rowlandson's sourcebook, interestingly also mentions a shrine to 'the Syrian goddess and Berenike Aphrodite' which her husband had built in their house before his death. Asia accuses her neighbour of preventing her from finishing the wall between their houses solely on account of her being widowed. One frustrating problem with the papyri is that we often never know the outcome of disputes or petitions because replies to letters have not been found.

With regard to land ownership, women were at a disadvantage because much of the royal land was allocated to Greek male soldiers in the form of allotments and officials were awarded larger 'gift' estates. It is interesting that outside the Faiyum, where the Greek immigrants were awarded this land, Egyptian women continued to own and work land. Women could also buy, sell, lease and inherit non-royal land and by the first century BC, if not before, they could also inherit the royal land that had been traditionally passed down to male relations.

Marriage, unlike that of the royals, was meant to be monogamous, and in fact a common feature of the marriage contract stipulates that neither party should marry a second person, nor live in a manner that might be construed as a marriage. This was doubtless intended to prevent questions over paternity and inheritance. It didn't always work, but this moral code would in theory at least discourage mistresses.

Divorce probably didn't always work in a woman's favour, but allowed her a degree of independence and certainly choice, as Ptolemaic women were permitted to petition for a legal separation from their husbands. In the Faiyum, it was not even necessary for a woman to give a reason for divorce, and the return of a woman's dowry was usual. Pomeroy notes that in Elephantine, in the south of Egypt, divorce settlements were somewhat of a lottery depending on which party was at fault. In this way, a wronged woman could walk away from a marriage with her dowry plus a considerable share of her husband's assets, but if she contravened the marriage contract then she would lose her dowry. Women in the papyri complain of abandonment and on occasion petition the king to ask that their wayward husbands should reimburse their dowries so that they too may be free to marry again.

Perhaps the most evocative image of women in Alexandria was a literary work by a man named Theocritus, who was a poet at the Mouseion in Alexandria during the reign of Ptolemy II, and who wrote an amusing idyll about two friends preparing to go to the royal palaces for a festival of Adonis. Praxinoa, one of the women, complains about her husband's choice of area in which to reside and his inability to buy two correct items on a shopping list when sent to the market on her behalf. The work may be fictitious, but it allows a wonderful insight into the adventure of two friends in preparation for, and attendance at, a festival. Like many of the women in the papyri, Praxinoa and her friend Gorgo are not women to suffer in silence. When compared to other ancient societies women fulfilled comprehensive roles in Ptolemaic Egypt, and had rights beyond those of women elsewhere in the Greek world. Women also had certain independence and were, it seems, free to go about their daily business alone and unescorted by a male. Many women were educated and certainly in Alexandria, as shown by Theocritus' poem, they enjoyed culture.

Women also held important roles such as that of priestess. In the Egyptian tradition, cult guilds (which were associations that seem to have functioned in many respects like a modern co-operative) could be exclusively female. Like other priestly positions in Egypt, there were hereditary female positions such as the libation bearers in cemeteries. Such positions enjoyed financial as well as social or religious rewards. However, life was not always easy for women involved in religious institutions, as illustrated most famously by the Memphite Sarapieion twins. Their life and catalogue of complaints against those who were meant to ensure basic provisions for these recluses is discussed fully by Thompson in her book *Memphis under the Ptolemies.* The twins were meant to fulfil the part of the Egyptian goddesses Isis and Nephthys during the mourning of the Apis bull. In a petition to Ptolemy VI dating to 163 BC, they complain about their mother, who absconded with a man and attempted to have her husband murdered. The papyrus notes that their father died of a broken heart, and that the mother wronged the twins further by throwing them out of the house and taking their possessions. The twins added further to their problems when they were persuaded to employ a relative of their mother as an attendant at the temple, and he stole all the property they had managed to obtain from their home. Such dysfunctional families were not, as we shall see, limited to the general population of Egypt; the Ptolemaic royal house often behaved in a similar way to the family of Thaues and Taous, the Sarapieion twins. The Ptolemies, however, petitioned Rome and rather than simply leave the area, from the mid-second century BC they temporarily fled the country. One further distinction that perhaps ought to be made is that there was certainly no love lost between many of the rulers and their queens.

CHAPTER 3

Cleopatra and her ancestors

The last queen

5 2–30 BC: Ptolemy XII Philopator; Ptolemy XIII; Ptolemy XIV; Ptolemy XV Caesar

The Ptolemaic period can be clearly defined between two deaths: that of Alexander the Great and that of Cleopatra VII and yet, historically, the treatment of these two figures, linked by not only their characters but also by their young deaths, is quite different. Alexander is held up as the gallant hero whereas Cleopatra is seen to be a licentious whore. It is for her beauty and her men that Cleopatra is most famed, and many people do not realise that she was a mother and ruler, or that she had a past as an individual. In spite of her skills as a diplomat and ruler, Cleopatra is famed for her love of men, when in actual fact two relationships in her 40 years is not excessive. Similarly, we forget to consider that she was a single mother who was twice rejected for marriage when the opportunity arose. Once by Julius Caesar when she was married to her younger brother, and then by Mark Antony who chose to marry Octavia (the sister of Octavian) even though he already had children with Cleopatra. When seen in this light and when we consider that she was forced to commit suicide at the age of 40, leaving her children behind her, we can suddenly see Cleopatra VII in a very different light.

With regard to her presentation, it is important to note that as far as Cleopatra was concerned, she would not be the last queen. In fact every part of her presentation, her foreign and domestic policies, were intended to re-establish the Ptolemaic dynasty as the sole survivors of the Hellenistic age. The names chosen for her sons with Mark Antony (Alexander and Ptolemy Philadelphos) illustrate her interest in associating with the past. Her re-acquisition of territories that had traditionally been part of the Ptolemaic empire, albeit through their donation by Mark Antony, also reveals a desire to return to the former glories of the dynasty. Cleopatra VII, who was actually the sixth Ptolemaic Cleopatra, is famed more for her men, her beauty and her death than for her policies. Without her liaisons, however, it is likely that Cleopatra VII would have become as anonymous as her predecessors.

In order to fully comprehend the impact of Cleopatra, we must, as the historian Hamer has done in her book *Signs of Cleopatra*, attempt to read between the lines of history. In Rome, the contempt of many leading Romans for her cannot have been solely on account of disdain. As ruler of Egypt, Cleopatra and her ability to court the powerful and influential Roman officials Julius Caesar and Mark Antony presented a threat to the Republic of Rome. Unlike her male predecessors, who ran to Rome in order to be placed back on their throne during periods of family feuding, Cleopatra came to the city at a time when she was in a strong position as ruler of Egypt and with a male child to continue the family line. Furthermore, a man who held as much power as was possible in a Republic fathered the child. Such diplomatic unions were commonplace among Cleopatra's predecessors and it is not impossible that she did not fully under-stand the reality of a Republic rather than sovereignty. There is little doubt, however, of her political prowess.

The question of Cleopatra's beauty is perhaps a truer reflec-tion of our society than many of its enquirers realise. The auto-matic assumption that it was her beauty rather than her leadership skills that enticed the two Romans is perhaps a poor reflection on their characters. It is interesting that Plutarch, in his *Life of Antony*, writes the following:

> Her own beauty, so we are told, was not of that incom-
> parable type that immediately captivates the beholder.
> But the charm of her presence was irresistible and there
> was an attraction in her person and in her conversation
> that, along with a peculiar force of character in her every
> word and action, laid all who associated with her under
> her spell. (Chapter 27)

Later, early Arab writers talk of her intelligence, and it is interesting to note that it was her intellect rather than her appearance
that was considered the essence of her beauty.

The ancient images of Cleopatra do not allow a realistic representation of her true appearance, and so it is futile to consider
whether such works represent a woman who was truly beautiful,
not least of all because beauty is by its definition both historically
and culturally bound. What is apparent from Cleopatra's images
is that she was a chameleon-like character who could be Greek
or Egyptian but never both at the same time. Her presentation
was divided not only according to form but also depending on
whether she was in Egypt or presenting herself to those abroad.
Cleopatra had a number of Egyptian role models on which to
model herself and her reign, and it is interesting that in terms of
the styles of many of her images she returns to the golden age of
the third century BC, a time when the Ptolemies were powerful
not only at home but also abroad.

In no form did Cleopatra appear visually as a male pharaoh,
although she is once called a pharaoh in a temple text. Unlike the
earlier queen Hatshepsut, Cleopatra was always shown in attire
suitable for a female member of the royal family, and unlike her
more immediate predecessor Cleopatra III, the last queen does
not seem to have adopted a masculine portrait type in Egypt.
Here, we see a deliberate play on the femininity of the queen, not
as a harlot but as a mother and personification of Isis as the
mother-goddess.

51

Indeed at home there was no place for either Julius Caesar or Mark Antony, because they were neither king nor pharaoh of Egypt. In Egypt we see Cleopatra presenting and promoting her son, Caesarion, in her images and with her dedications. A male consort was essential, as Cleopatra Berenike found out to her peril when the Romans insisted on her taking a husband, by whom she was killed. Having fought off two brothers it seems unlikely that Cleopatra VII would have been willing to adopt a co-regent or consort who had any political power. Cleopatra's Egyptian consorts are confusing to say the least, for even when an inscription accompanies a statue or relief representation the similarity in titles makes it difficult to distinguish between her father, brothers and son. Cleopatra probably linked visually to her consorts of choice, her father and son. On her Greek-style portraits she adopted the harsh features of her father's official portrait type, and in the Egyptian-style representations the queen is linked to a male figure, most probably her son, who is often shown as a young prince with a diadem. This visual link was, as previously noted, also promoted on temple walls; most notably on the south wall of the temple of Hathor at Denderah (Figure 3).

In some respects, however, we see a confusing message when we consider that Caesarion only appeared with his mother on the coins from Cyprus, which were probably minted to celebrate his birth. In Egypt Cleopatra generally appears alone. On only one occasion, however, does Antony play a key role in Egyptian cere-mony, at the Donations of Alexandria. During this ceremony, held in 34 BC, Roman possessions were returned to the Ptolemaic empire and each of the children was allocated a region. Caesarion was named as Julius Caesar's rightful heir and Cleopatra was named Queen of Kings. The ceremony, which was described in Plutarch's *Life of Antony*, was on all accounts a splendid event which involved the Alexandrians; this was a return to the early pompes of the Ptolemies both in form and in its promotion of the royal family. It was during this ceremony that Cleopatra was named the New Isis, perhaps to distinguish

Figure 3   Temple relief showing Cleopatra and Caesarion, Denderah.
(Photograph and copyright Sally-Ann Ashton.)

53

her from her predecessor Cleopatra III, or to emulate her father who had been the New Dionysos. What is perhaps most interesting about the event is that, in Egyptian terms, Cleopatra is shown to be ruler. The seating arrangements that are described by Plutarch place the children on thrones below those of Cleopatra and Mark Antony. It is probably unlikely that Antony was here shown as the queen's consort but that the two acted as heads of state; Cleopatra as ruler of Egypt and Mark Antony of Rome.

The queen's relationship with Mark Antony was publicised on the coins, possibly minted in Antioch, where one appears on each side and where both rulers adopt portrait features which emulate those of Ptolemy XII; Cleopatra, here, appearing with masculine features. On the coins we see an important public alliance celebrated and promoted on arguably the best method of advertising available in the ancient world. Cleopatra would have been comfortable with her position as ruler of Syria because of her family connections, not least of all with the infamous Cleopatra Thea, with whom she shared Arsinoe II's double cornucopia in her iconography.

Part of Cleopatra's reputation is, of course, linked to her suicide, and several scholars have postulated as to whether her death by the poison of an asp (which is more likely to have been an Egyptian cobra) wasn't linked to her status as queen. This seems, however, to be quite perverse given that the uraeus or cobra was meant to protect the royals as a representation of the eye of Horus. Griffiths, in an article published in the *Journal of Egyptian Archaeology*, suggested that the statues with a double uraeus could be linked to Cleopatra VII on account of her death, suggesting that the queen would have required two snakes to kill herself and the two servants who accompanied her in the mausoleum chamber. Although less romantic, it would seem far more sensible to administer poison straight into the bloodstream rather than risk the snake not biting when required to do so. There would also have been the problem of concealing one or more snakes. Such risks seem unlikely for a woman who meticulously planned all other aspects of her life, but the legend of

Figure 4 *Cleopatra cigarettes. (Photograph and copyright Sally-Ann Ashton.)*

Cleopatra lives on and Ptolemaic historians owe a debt to the queen, for if nothing else she provides credibility to a period that is often neglected.

Cleopatra VII is the most commonly adopted queen in modern-day Egypt. Her name adorns the most popular brand of cigarette (Figure 4), tours, household goods and even hotels and restaurants. She is also shown, appropriately for her own policies, as an Egyptian queen and is held as a national figure.

In many respects the Ptolemaic queens are tragic historical figures. While we gasp at their antics and the horrors that they suffered in order to maintain control of Egypt, it is often difficult to remember that these were real people with real lives. At the same time, without them the history of the Ptolemaic dynasty would not have been quite so interesting. They may have been used by their fathers, brothers and consorts for their own self-promotion, but the queens achieved a status that is rare for women in either the Greek or Egyptian world, most notably because their wilfulness was passed on from mother to daughter, or quickly learnt by those who found themselves thrown into the vipers' nest that the Ptolemaic royal house soon became.

Euridike

323–287 BC: Ptolemy I Soter

Euridike was Ptolemy I's second wife, to whom he was still married when Berenike I had her first child, Arsinoe II, with the ruler. Ironically, the eldest of Euridike's six children, Ptolemy Keraunos, played an important but disturbing role in the life of Arsinoe II. Like most points of contact between members of the Ptolemaic royal family, such associations were far from cordial affairs. Euridike and Keraunos, the rightful heir to the Egyptian throne, were exiled around 287 BC.

Berenike I

323-–? BC: Ptolemy I Soter

Ptolemy I was not Berenike's first husband. The queen had previously married Philip of Macedonia, and with him she had a child called Magas, who became ruler of Cyrenaica in modern Libya. Magas's only child, a daughter, would marry Ptolemy III and become Berenike II. Berenike I also became the third wife of Ptolemy I and mother of: his successor, Ptolemy II, who was born in 308 BC; Arsinoe II, who was the eldest child, born in 316 BC; another girl Philoteira; and possibly a fourth child.

Arsinoe I

?300–275 BC: Ptolemy II Philadelphos

Arsinoe I, and not the better-known second queen with this name, was the mother of Ptolemy II's children, including the future pharaoh Ptolemy III Euergetes. The queen was the daughter of Lysimachos of Thrace, who was married to Arsinoe II. Following Arsinoe II's marriage in 275 BC, the first queen was exiled to Koptos in Upper Egypt, where she remained until her death. For the Egyptians her exile must have seemed an unnecessary act because Egyptian rulers typically had more than one wife. There is evidence of statues representing the queen during her early years in Egypt, but her presence was shadowed following the return of Arsinoe II.

Arsinoe II

275–270 BC: Ptolemy II Philadelphos

Arsinoe II was an exceptional woman and can, in many respects, be seen as a pioneer for later queens. In 300 BC, at the age of 16, she was married to Lysimachos, ruler of Thrace who was 44 years her senior. In exchange, Lysimachos' daughter, also named Arsinoe (who became Arsinoe I of Egypt), was married to Ptolemy II. In 283/2 BC Arsinoe II arranged for the murder of Agathokles, who was the rightful heir of her husband. His widow, who was the half-sister of Arsinoe II, fled with her children to another court at Samothrace, and having routed support among other dissidents and supporters of Agathokles, Ptolemy II wages a war against Lysimachos in which the latter lost his life in 281 BC. Arsinoe, in what can perhaps be interpreted as an attempt to secure survival for herself and her children by Lysimachos, then married Ptolemy Keraunos who promptly killed her two sons, but allowed the queen to flee. Following the murder of her children, she returned to Egypt around 279 BC. Ptolemy II chose, or was persuaded by Arsinoe II from around 275 BC, to have a single consort; that was not to say that the ruler didn't have mistresses – in fact, their accommodation was legendary for its decadent setting. To Egyptians this arrangement would not have been out of the ordinary, and indeed there had been earlier sibling marriages, or marriages between father and daughter. For Greeks, however, the idea of a brother–sister marriage was abhorrent. The double defiance of self-deification and a sibling marriage may in an odd way have eased the blow for Greeks; the one making the other more acceptable. Such was the power of Arsinoe II that Ptolemy III appears on temple reliefs making offerings to his 'parents', Ptolemy II and Arsinoe II. Arsinoe remained an important focal point and role model for the women of the dynasty, and her cult remained popular into the Roman period.

Berenike II

246–222/1 BC: Ptolemy III Euergetes I

Arsinoe II's successor was, as previously noted, part Ptolemaic. Berenike I, wife of Ptolemy I, had originally married Philip of Macedonia, by whom she had had a son, Magas king of Cyrene; Magas was therefore the half-brother of Ptolemy II and Arsinoe II. Berenike II was the only child from Magas's marriage to Apame (herself a daughter of Antiochus I, a Seleucid ruler). In true Ptolemaic fashion the ancient literary sources tell of the princess's murder of her intended husband, a young Macedonian ruler called Demetrius the Fair. During her father's lifetime Berenike had been promised to Ptolemy III, supposedly in an attempt to unify the two kingdoms of Egypt and Cyrenaica. Following the death of Magas, however, queen Apame decided that it would be better for Cyrenaica to remain independent and so arranged for a suitable husband to be brought to the city. After finding her prospective husband in her mother's bedroom, it is said by Justin (26.3) that Berenike had Demetrius murdered and was then able to fulfil her original betrothal to Ptolemy III. Plutarch (*Demetrius* 53), however, states that Demetrius was king, which would imply that the two were married. Either way the story is typical of the Ptolemaic rulers and Berenike would, no doubt, have fitted easily within the Alexandrian royal court.

Berenike, as queen, owned her own racing horses and land thus allowing her some independence. The literary sources recount her going into battle beside her husband and note that she was a keen horse-woman. Such attributes are perhaps to be expected given that she was the only child of Magas and Apame and are characteristics that other Ptolemaic women are cited to have had. To what extent the queen literally went into battle is not known; the *Lock of Berenike*, which was a poem written by Theocritus in honour of the queen, implies that the queen waited for her husband to return from war and indeed, politically, it would have made more sense for her to stay at home during her husband's campaigns overseas in order to keep control not only over Egypt, but also over those members of the Alexandrian court who had aspirations of power.

Berenike II seems to have been genuinely close to Ptolemy III and, in fact, they had six children, compared to Ptolemy IV and Arsinoe III who had one child. The aforementioned *Lock of Berenike* describes her dedication of a lock of hair in the temple of Arsinoe, for the safe return of her husband from the Syrian wars. Here, Berenike is shown as a caring queen, and references to the usual marital feuds are not found with regard to this couple. Berenike is also shown as a mother figure, most especially in association with the princess Berenike, who died at a young age and was subsequently deified. Her own fate, however, was not as calm as her marriage and rule. Following the death of her husband, she was murdered when the 20-year-old Ptolemy IV came to the throne. Polybios (*Histories* V.34.1, 36.1 and XV.25.1–2) states that Sosibios, an adviser to Ptolemy IV and a man whose name would later be associated with further murders, was responsible. It is hard to see how Ptolemy IV, who was by this time twenty years of age, could not have known about this plan, and it is also easy to see how he could benefit from the eradication of potential rivals to his throne. He took the title *Philopator* or father-loving, but later promoted the cult of his mother. Whether this was through a genuine regret, self-promotion or respect is difficult to know. Sosibios maintained a high profile in the Alexandrian court.

Arsinoe III

222–204 BC: Ptolemy IV Philopator

Ancient historians such as Polybios blamed Ptolemy IV for the downfall of the dynasty on account of his licentious and decadent behaviour. As heir to the throne he was married to the youngest child and his full sister, Arsinoe III. Arsinoe appears to have been long suffering and the fact that the couple only had one child is probably representative of their marriage. Whereas Ptolemy IV was shown as Dionysos, a suitable god for someone who was fond of extravagant parties, one scholar described Arsinoe's portrait as reminiscent of that of a Victorian maid. Her biographer, Eratosthenes, recounted a story of the queen lamenting at the palace gates on account of her brother's constant, drunken gatherings. On temples and stelae Arsinoe III appears alongside her brother. On all of the versions of the Raphia decree she stands behind Ptolemy IV, who smites his enemy while riding a horse, and she also appears on the so-called Apotheosis of Homer by the artist Archelaos, which is now in the British Museum: standing with a kalathos or grain measure on her head, emphasising her role as provider and mother of Egypt, Arsinoe is shown placing the crown on the head of Homer. In this role she must have been perceived as a goddess since she is creating a god. And yet in other areas Ptolemy IV replaces images of his queen with those of his mother and himself. However, it was not only in visual terms that Arsinoe III was ostracised.

Ptolemy IV had a powerful mistress called Agathokleia, who was the sister of one of the members of the court, Agathokles. Agathokles was close to Sosibius, who it should be remembered had murdered the king's immediate family, sparing Arsinoe III for a royal marriage. Ptolemy IV died unexpectedly in 204 BC leaving Arsinoe with a 6-year-old son who was too young to rule but was the rightful heir to the throne. This was the perfect opportunity for Sosibios and his supporters to take charge of the king and Egypt; Arsinoe III was murdered and the joint deaths of Ptolemy IV Philopator and his queen were announced to the

Alexandrians. Shortly after this episode Sosibios died, leaving Agathokles and Agathokleia in charge of the young Ptolemy V. It was not long before word leaked out, and a year later the Alexandrians revolted, killing Agathokles and his family in public, in the stadium. The mother, a woman named Oinanthe, fled to the temple of Demeter, but was dragged out by the mob, stripped and led to the stadium on horseback, where she was publicly executed.

Cleopatra I

194/3–176 BC: Ptolemy V Epiphanes; Ptolemy VI Philometor

It is perhaps of no surprise that when Ptolemy V came of age in 196 BC, he moved the royal court back to Memphis. In 195 BC Ptolemy, who took the title *Epiphanes*, became engaged to a Syrian princess called Cleopatra. This deal had been struck following the Fifth Syrian War, in which Antiochus III, ruler of Syria, seized Ptolemaic territories. When told by Rome that he had to hand them back, he retorted that he had good relations with Egypt and that his daughter was to marry its ruler Ptolemy V. In 194/3 BC the couple married in Raphia; he was 16 years of age and she was about 10. In a papyrus dating to 191/190 BC, Cleopatra, who was not it must be remembered a blood relation of Ptolemy V, was described as 'his sister and his wife', thus continuing the idea of sibling marriage in the Ptolemaic tradition. It would seem odd if this were an error by the scribe and here it seems to have been part of the formal titulature; this association must then have been a deliberate reference to her ritual role within the dynastic cult. Later in the dynasty non-siblings were also called sister of the king, perhaps in an attempt to strengthen the position of the rulers by associating themselves with a more successful period of the dynasty's history.

Cleopatra I and Ptolemy V had three children, two boys and a girl. Each was power-hungry and ruthless, and the stories that have come down through the ancient written sources are at times beyond belief. The youngest, who was without doubt the worst perpetrator, was given the nick-name *Physcon* or fatty, and although his images at first sight appear to reveal a chubby, affable character, the literary sources reveal nothing less than a monster. Some historians have postulated that his obesity and character may have been the result of inbreeding, but as Cleopatra I was from foreign stock, this hypothesis can hardly be supported. It seems more likely that the younger son looked to his grandfather, Ptolemy IV, for a role model.

Epiphanes died in 180 BC, aged 30. Diodorus Siculus writing in the first century BC (XXIX.9.7) states that Ptolemy V was poisoned by his generals after threatening to take their money to fight a military campaign overseas. Cleopatra was only 24 years of age and her eldest son was 6 years old. Rather than the usual pattern of events, however, Cleopatra was officially declared regent to her son. Her supremacy is noted in the dating formulae of this period, where she is named before her son and takes the title *Thea* or goddess. Coins were also minted in her honour, showing the queen's veiled image on one side and her son, Ptolemy VI, on the other. This association is a direct link to the earlier queens of Egypt who ruled with their sons, and to the promotion of 'king's mother'. Such was the relationship between Cleopatra I and her son, Ptolemy VI, that when he took a cult title it was *Philometor* or mother-loving. During her rule, Cleopatra showed herself to be a skilled diplomat. She maintained good relations with the Seleucids in Syria and her brother, who was a contemporary ruler.

Cleopatra II

175–116 BC: Ptolemy VI Philometor; Ptolemy VIII Euergetes II; Cleopatra III

Cleopatra II was arguably one of the most powerful Ptolemaic queens. In 175 BC she married her brother Ptolemy VI Philometor who was 10 or 11 years of age. However, in 170 BC it was decided by the regents in charge of the royal children that Ptolemy VI and Cleopatra II should be joined by their younger brother Ptolemy VIII Euergetes II as part of a triple rule. Then, Alexandrians, following the invasion of Egypt by Syrian forces, decided to put the younger brother alone on the throne. According to Livy (XLIV.19.9 and 19.12), Cleopatra II remained queen, thus illustrating the strength of a female consort's position. A year later, all three were back on the throne, and the triple rule lasted until 164/3 when Ptolemy VI was again exiled. When he returned Ptolemy VIII was ousted and sent to Cyprus, and remained there until the death of Ptolemy VI.

For the remainder of Ptolemy VI's reign he ruled with Cleopatra II as queen. The pair had four children, the eldest of whom, Ptolemy Eupator, was declared co-regent with his father in 152 BC. He died suddenly later that year. There were two girls, both called Cleopatra (Thea and the future Cleopatra III), and a boy whose name was not recorded. The girls became two of the most powerful women of the Ptolemaic period, no doubt as a result of their mother's influence.

Ptolemy VI died fighting in a foreign campaign in 145 BC. His brother wasted no time in seizing the Ptolemaic throne, marrying Cleopatra II in 145/4 BC and according to Justin (XXXVIII.8.4), murdering the rightful heir to the throne, the youngest son, in his mother's arms during the marriage celebrations. In 144 BC Cleopatra II gave birth to a son, Ptolemy Memphites, and shortly after the birth Ptolemy VIII started a relationship with his niece, Cleopatra III.

In 141/0 BC, Ptolemy VIII took a second wife, marrying his niece and the daughter of his sister and first wife; Cleopatra III was already the mother of her uncle's child. This was the first time that a Ptolemy had taken two wives, unlike earlier pharaonic multiple marriages; however, both were equal and there was no 'principal wife' as such. However, Ptolemy VIII clearly found his niece less troublesome and it was her children that would succeed to the throne.

Thus, for the second time in Ptolemaic history there were three rulers on the throne. The second triple-rule was no happier than the first, which is of little surprise given that two of the former regime were part of the new. Added to this was a daughter who proved to have a stronger personality than her mother, although it is hard to fully comprehend the awkwardness of the situation in which the pair found themselves. The three ruled – not always together – from 145 to 116 BC. Cleopatra II was referred to as 'the sister' and Cleopatra III as 'the wife'.

In 139 BC a supporter of Cleopatra II attempted, unsuccessfully, to invade Egypt. This was not the last time that the brother and sister would oppose each other; in 132 BC a civil war broke out and supporters were split between the royal pair. Ptolemy fled to Cyprus with his younger wife and sent for his son by his sister: Ptolemy Memphites. Cleopatra II was declared sole ruler of Egypt and started a new reign in 132/1 BC with a new dating formula. Realising that his heir, who was now 14 years of age, was in fact his greatest threat to regaining his throne, Ptolemy VIII witnessed the murder of his son. As a warning to his sister he sent the dismembered body to Alexandria where it was delivered to the queen during her birthday celebrations. Not one to miss a PR exercise, Cleopatra II put the body parts on display, so that her subjects could see her brother's true character. The queen had now lost two sons to her brother's wrath.

Cleopatra III

141/40–101 BC: Ptolemy VIII Euergetes II; Cleopatra II; Ptolemy IX Soter II; Ptolemy X Alexander

Cleopatra III bore five children to her uncle: two boys, who would carry on the dynastic feuding, and three girls. Following the murder of Memphites, the elder boy was declared heir to the throne. Both he and his brother would rule on the throne of Egypt and like their father they were both called *Physcon* on account of their large proportions. Of the girls, the eldest, Tryphaina, was married to Antiochos VIII; the second, who became Cleopatra IV, married her elder brother, and the youngest was called Cleopatra Selene. In addition to the legitimate children there was a boy called Ptolemy Apion, who went on to rule Cyrenaica, later bequeathing the territory to Rome as his father had once promised in an attempt to gain support.

When Ptolemy VIII died in 116 BC, he stated in his will that his younger wife should rule Egypt with whichever son she wished. Although at first such a power may seem like a liberating gift, it is hard to envisage a more difficult and indeed potentially dangerous situation for the queen. Her mother, who by this time must have had a strained relationship with her daughter, was still alive and politically active. It was decided that Ptolemy IX should be sent to Cyprus and that Ptolemy X, the younger son, should rule with his mother. The Alexandrians refused to accept this situation and so the elder brother became Ptolemy IX Soter II. At this point Cleopatra II died, leaving her daughter in control. Perhaps by way of punishment or for political reasons, Cleopatra III decided that her son should marry his youngest sister Cleopatra Selene rather than Cleopatra IV to whom he was already married. The second union took place in 115 BC. It should perhaps have been obvious that the deposed Cleopatra IV would have fled to her other brother in Cyprus, which indeed she did. Rather than forming a long-term alliance with the exiled Ptolemy X, she went to the Syrian ruler Antiochos IX. It should be remembered that Tryphaina, who was the sister of Cleopatra IV, had been married to Antiochos IX's brother and arch-enemy Antiochos VIII. What followed was a particularly vicious dispute between two lots of siblings. Antiochos IX was victorious and seized power in 114/13 BC, but his wife Cleopatra IV was left in charge of the royal palaces in Antioch. Antiochos VIII returned to the city and took control of it in his brother's absence. At Tryphaina's orders, her sister Cleopatra IV was taken from the sanctuary in which she was hiding, and as she clung to the cult statue her hands were chopped off.

Cleopatra III clearly wanted to rule with her younger son and finally in 107 BC her wish was granted and Ptolemy X Alexander became ruler of Egypt. The supplanting of the younger Ptolemy was a dramatic affair at which Cleopatra announced to the

Alexandrians that her elder son, Ptolemy IX, had tried to kill her. According to the writer Pausanias, the queen had had some of her guards beaten and shown to the crowd in order to authenticate the story. The mob then attacked Ptolemy IX, who escaped to Cyprus, and once again the two brothers swapped roles. Cleopatra III entered into an alliance with the Seleucid Antiochos VIII by offering her daughter Cleopatra Selene, who was also Ptolemy IX's wife, to replace the murdered Tryphaina. The family feuds continued with Cleopatra III and Ptolemy X victorious, and Ptolemy IX exiled once again in Cyprus. In 101 BC, however, Cleopatra III died. Some ancient sources allege that her son, Ptolemy X, who had perhaps tired of his mother, had her murdered.

Cleopatra Berenike

101–80 BC: Ptolemy X Alexander I; Ptolemy IX Soter II; Ptolemy XI Alexander II

Berenike III was taken by her uncle Ptolemy X as a replacement for Cleopatra III, becoming Cleopatra Berenike, thus continuing the family name. Although she was not the ruler's sister, she is referred to as such in texts. In 88 BC, however, Ptolemy X was deposed; he had apparently become the model of his father – licentious, overweight and proved to be a weak ruler without his mother. Ptolemy IX returned to the throne and took Cleopatra Berenike, his daughter, as his consort. Father–daughter marriages had their roots in dynastic Egypt with Akhenaten and Ramesses II taking their daughters as consorts. Some historians have suggested that Ptolemy IX retained his daughter as queen because she was popular with the Alexandrians; others point to the fact that there was not an obvious alternative. In 81 BC Ptolemy IX died and Cleopatra Berenike was given sole charge of Egypt, ruling in her own right for six months until June 80 BC when Rome decided that Egypt needed a male pharaoh on the throne. The son of Ptolemy X and nephew of Cleopatra Berenike was chosen and became Ptolemy XI

Alexander II; his mother is unknown. In true Ptolemaic fashion, Ptolemy XI decided that he wanted sole power and murdered his new wife after less than three weeks of marriage. Once again the Alexandrian mob rose against their king, and he was dragged out and executed in the stadium.

Cleopatra Tryphaina

80–57 (?)BC: Ptolemy XII Philopator; Cleopatra Berenike IV

Following the disastrous rule of Ptolemy XI, a son of Ptolemy IX was chosen as ruler: Ptolemy XII Philopator, who was married to his sister Cleopatra Tryphaina. Their mother is unknown, and the fact that Ptolemy XII was known as *nothos* or bastard among other nick-names, which included *Auletes* (the flute-player), might suggest that he was illegitimate. A third child from this union was also called Ptolemy, who ruled in Cyprus.

Cleopatra Tryphaina and Ptolemy XII had at least one child, a girl called Cleopatra Berenike IV. Scholars are divided as to the identity of the mother of the other children, and although traditionally Cleopatra Tryphaina is thought to have been the mother of all of Ptolemy XII's other children, Hölbl has recently questioned this supposition. These children were Arsinoe, Cleopatra (who would become the VIIth and most famous queen) and two boys who would become Ptolemy XIII and Ptolemy XIV. The queen appears to have ruled with her daughter, Cleopatra Berenike IV, for one year.

Cleopatra Berenike IV

58–55 BC: Cleopatra Tryphaina

Cleopatra Berenike IV ruled with Cleopatra Tryphaina in 58/7 BC and there is documentary evidence for a rule of 'queens'. It is here that the confusion over the numbering of the Cleopatras occurs because the writer Porphyry states that the co-ruler of Berenike was not her mother but another sister called

Cleopatra Tryphaina, hence she would be Cleopatra VI Tryphaina. As Whitehorne notes, however, there is little evidence to support the sixth Cleopatra. The problem is exacerbated by the fact that Cleopatra V Tryphaina disappears from documents in 69/8 BC but reappears on the Temple of Horus at Edfu in 57 BC. In a time where cartouches are often left blank, however, her missing name would hardly seem to be a case for her death. After a year of co-rule then, Cleopatra V Tryphaina died in 57 BC and Cleopatra Berenike needed a husband. There were several candidates, and one who claimed to be from the Syrian Seleucid line was brought to Alexandria, but the literary sources claim that the queen disliked him on account of his character and had him strangled. In 56 BC, however, Cleopatra Berenike married Archelaos, who claimed to be the son of the ruler Mithradates VI. The queen was put to death following the return of her exiled father in 55 BC. In her place, in 52 BC, Ptolemy XII took his other daughter Cleopatra VII as his co-ruler; a year later, following his death, his will stated that Rome should supervise the joint rule of Ptolemy XIII and Cleopatra VII. Cleopatra was 18 years old at the time of her father's death and her brother was 12; she left no doubt as to her status or allegiance, taking the title Cleopatra *Thea* (goddess) and *Philopator* (father-loving).

CHAPTER 4

Presentation to the Greeks: Hellenistic queens

The Ptolemaic royal women may have been the last queens of Egypt, but they were by descent Macedonian Greeks. On their Greek-style portraits we find quite distinct portrait types, which although idealised in the usual Greek fashion offer an insight into the personalities of the queens. At the same time they often hint at the queen's divinity by following the known appearance of goddesses such as Aphrodite and Artemis. Such individualisation stands in contrast to Egyptian images of early Ptolemaic queens, which with the exception of Arsinoe II, are difficult to distinguish between.

Coinage was used as a means of promoting the current royal image. The obvious advantage of coin portraits to modern scholars is that they are often inscribed with the name of the ruler whose portrait they carry, and so it is possible to establish portrait types for each king to compare with the sculpture in the round. Coins functioned not only as money in circulation, but also, as Smith suggests, to remind the armies that the king paid their wages; this accounts for one particular function of the royal image. Coins also provide a convenient way of familiarising the literate wealthy members of communities with the image adopted by a particular ruler, so that at least some of the population would recognise a ruler's portrait in religious or political contexts.

Unlike the early kings, the first Ptolemaic queens only appeared posthumously on coinage. From 285–246 BC Ptolemy II minted gold coins with an image of Ptolemy I and Berenike I as the Theoi Soteres on one side and himself with Arsinoe II as the Theoi Adelphoi on the other. These images sent a strong message of dynastic alliance and also served to promote the current ruler, Ptolemy II, alongside his divine parents and sibling. The 'portraits' of the two queens are virtually indistinguishable and it is the inscription at the top of the image that enables the viewer to identify the subjects. Here the queens are little more than an accessory. However, on coins minted specifically in their honour the queens are awarded a greater autonomy, in terms of an identifiable portrait type and specific iconography. On coins minted in her name by her consort, Berenike II is shown with a fuller face than her predecessor, also a characteristic of her sculpted portraits. This queen wears a veil and diadem and on the reverse there is a single cornucopia with a royal diadem wrapped around the top. The title 'Queen Berenike' is also stamped on the back, indicating her status when the coin was minted, and showing that this was during her lifetime. This royal image contrasts with that of her consort, who appears on his own coins with the crown of the sun god Helios, the aegis of Zeus and the trident of Neptune, the god of the sea. Nevertheless, the queen's solitary appearance is evidence of her independence. The promotion of divine queens will be discussed further in Chapter 6.

In addition to indicating the status of the Ptolemaic royal women, the coins are helpful in other ways. They help with the identification of royal images on finger-rings or seals and also on the clay impressions made from them. The differences between the widely circulated coinage and the more select official seals or items of jewellery are of considerable interest. A large collection of clay seal impressions was found at Edfu in Upper Egypt and was split between two museums: the Allard Pierson Museum in Amsterdam and the Royal Ontario Museum in Toronto. The so-called Edfu hoard consists of different types: royal, divine, and the names of priests written in a hieroglyphic script. The reed impressions at the back of many of the sealings indicate that they were once used to seal papyrus documents. Those with images of the Ptolemaic royal women show later examples of two or three rulers in a jugate position, similar in fact to the early coins of Ptolemy II showing his parents on one side and he and his sister-wife on the reverse. The back two images appear to be female and the rulers wear Egyptian crowns. There is also one example from the Royal Ontario Museum, which shows a possible portrait of Ptolemy XII with a female consort, possibly Cleopatra V or VII. Individual queens also appear on the sealings, one particularly fine example shows a portrait of Cleopatra VII wearing a vulture headdress and Egyptian wig. Unlike the coins, these images were not reserved for Greek consumption. Several finger-rings illustrate the idealised portraits of the early queens, with their hair styled in a bun, and there was a continuous stream into the second century BC, where corkscrew locks show divine queens. Finger-rings also indicate a wider range of iconographical features, including representations of the queens as Egyptian goddesses. Some of this category show a masculine portrait type and probably represent Cleopatra II or III, and examples that may well represent the more rounded, idealised portrait features of Cleopatra VII. Officials or simply supporters of the royal house may have owned such objects, many of which were manufactured in gold.

There are a surprising number of small marble heads of Ptolemaic queens, of an idealised and general nature. These heads, without attributes, are easily confused with representations of Greek deities. While this in itself is instructive, demonstrating a further link between the royal house and the gods, the heads are of such a general nature that it is impossible to distinguish between rulers and it is often necessary simply to label pieces either third or second century BC. This type of dedication was probably made on behalf of the royal house and is no doubt associated with the faience cult vases, showing portraits of queens.

Figure 5 *Faience cult vase with a representation of Arsinoe II. (The British Museum Department of Greek and Roman Antiquities K77. Copyright and reproduced with permission of The British Museum.)*

These vases are a useful resource for both portrait types and iconography because they are decorated with a full-length portrait of the queen (Figure 5). Interestingly the vases were only produced for a limited period between the reigns of Ptolemy II and Ptolemy IV (285 to 204 BC), and thus the queens they show are Arsinoe II, Berenike II and Arsinoe III. Like the images on coins, some of the cult vases were manufactured contemporaneously, and others posthumously in honour of the deceased queen. There are certain clues, however, which greatly aid identification of individuals. Firstly, the contemporary images are likely to show the queen with a diadem or royal band around her head, whereas the images of goddesses and deified queens are identified as such by the *stephane* or crown. The vases offer an interesting insight into the role of Ptolemaic queens in the presentation of the dynasty from the third to the second century BC. They also give an impression of how some of the complete statues would have appeared. The images show the queen in Hellenistic costume with Greek attributes; in one hand they hold a cornucopia symbolising the fruits of Egypt and their role as provider, in the other they pour a libation from a bowl. It has been suggested that the small marble heads of queens were used in a similar way, in sanctuaries that were connected with the royal cult, possibly even by the second century BC, representing the individual queen's own cult or that which was connected with the ruler. The link between coins and cult vases and presumably statues, when they were complete, illustrates a carefully planned and interlinked iconography, which was then adopted by Egyptian artists for a culturally mixed audience. The queens played an important role in religion and politics and a survey of the development of their Greek-style images displays this point well.

The find-spot of a statue is important for our knowledge of the spread of Greek royal images and the intended audience to which they were addressed. Traditionally Alexandria, as capital, has been seen as the main centre for Greek culture and as such has been a focus for scholars of the classical world. Recent excavations, however, have cast considerable doubt on the Greek character of the city, particularly from the early second century BC and the reign of Cleopatra I. The Greco-Roman Museum, which now houses the city's collections of Greek, Roman and Egyptian art, has become a repository for non-Egyptian material found elsewhere in Egypt and, as a consequence, the modern visitor has a somewhat biased impression of the character of the ancient city. Unfortunately, due to the archaeological methods of the past, many objects have lost their original provenance and it is not always possible to know where or how an individual representation of a ruler was used in its original context. We do, however, have some Greek-style representations of queens, which are known to be from Alexandria and from other sites in the Delta.

The Greek-style portraits are in many respects the most frustrating group of royal representations from Ptolemaic Egypt. The poor survival rate of the Greek-style sculptures is in some cases due to the nature of their design. Sculptors often produced only the head of an image in marble, finishing off the details in stucco (plaster); the body of the statue and indeed any attributes would have been manufactured in a different and generally perishable or recyclable material, such as wood, precious metal, ivory or bronze. Consequently the modern scholar has very little diagnostic detail to help with the identification of individual pieces, particularly those without a context.

The practice of manufacturing the body and head separately may have evolved because of a lack of good-quality marble from Egypt. On the other hand, certain types of marble were highly prized and appropriate for Greek-style images of the royal family and gods. There may have been little difference between the cost of importing larger pieces of marble from Ptolemaic possessions or via trade and the cost of producing a statue in gold or ivory, which illustrates a specific desire to use marble for the royal image. The only white marble is found in Gebel Rokham (east of Esna and two-thirds of the way between the Nile and the Red Sea), and it is not known if the quarries were exploited in the

Ptolemaic times. Pliny (*Natural Histories*, xxxvi.67) mentions a marble called Memphites, after Memphis, although it has been suggested that this may not have been a true marble, but hard limestone. The fashion for composite sculpture may also have been influenced by the temporary art from the many festivals and processions that were held in Alexandria. Presumably the art that was manufactured for the processions, as described by Kallixeinos of Rhodes in Athenaeus' *Deipnosophistai*, would have been placed in public areas following the celebrations. This action would serve as a lasting reminder of the lavish festivals that were held in the capital, and also perhaps as a display for those who had missed the event by way of offering an impression of the original festival. It is also possible that sculptures were dedicated at temples around the city following the festival.

What do the surviving portrait types tell us about the early Ptolemaic queens, and how do the images accord with our knowledge of their lives through the historical and literary sources? Firstly, it is important to note that 'portrait' is a loaded term as, today, we expect a portrait to offer a realistic representation of the subject. Here, portrait is used to mean a recognisable representation, in other words the Greek-style heads are no more representative of the queen's appearance than those on Egyptian statues. Greek artists simply used a different set of artistic canons and tradition on which to draw, and as models for images of individuals. Greek-style representations may appear to the modern western eye as a truer likeness but this is rarely the case, particularly with regard to images of women, which are typically idealised.

The Hellenistic Greek-style portraits of Ptolemaic queens raise two main questions: firstly, whether the lost bodies of statues contained any Egyptian or Egyptianising elements and, secondly, whether individual pieces were intended for sanctuaries or public places – in other words, whether they served a political, decorative or religious purpose. It is in this respect that the images on coinage and sealings are particularly useful, because, although only the bust is shown, the rulers are often adorned with various attributes of either royal or divine nature. The portraits in these media, although miniature and stylised, offer an impression of a ruler's portrait type, although the coins need to be used with a degree of caution since many images are posthumous.

Scholars traditionally identify marble portrait heads by comparison with the profile images on coins. One of the main problems with this method of identification is the discrepancy in size and medium, but perhaps another more important difficulty is that the coin images of individual queens are posthumous because they were minted in their honour. On the coins showing a portrait of the queen alongside, or behind, the profile of the ruler, the women adopt the same portrait features, which are also, as noted, of a general nature. This potentially creates a problem when attempting to identify the marble heads, because they are uninscribed fragments and there is nothing to indicate whether the portrait we are looking at is contemporary with the queen's life or, in some cases, considerably later.

There are no identified portraits of Berenike I in the round. In fact the queen does not appear alone, but is typically shown behind the image of Ptolemy I Soter in a jugate position. Such images can be found on posthumous coins of the Theoi Soteres and on a relief in Alexandria depicting the royal pair, which shows the queen with rounded face, very similar to that of Soter. The lack of representations of Berenike I mirrors the scarcity of those of her consort Ptolemy I, and Ptolemaic Egypt's first royal couple were perhaps eclipsed by the popularity of the cult of Arsinoe II, assiduously promoted by Ptolemy II and Ptolemy III. In many ways Arsinoe II seems to have been the dynasty's most prominent female, and this is reflected by the number of surviving posthumous representations created throughout the period and also by Ptolemy III's adoption of Arsinoe as his mother.

It is of little surprise that our evidence for Greek-style royal representations comes from areas known to have had Greek communities, including Alexandria. The evidence for the

Figure 6 Unfinished head of a queen or goddess from Alexandria. (Greco-Roman Museum, Alexandria 31877. Photograph by Sally-Ann Ashton.)

development of Alexandrian royal image comes from two sources: from sanctuaries such as the Sarapieion – the cult itself an artificial amalgam of Egyptian and Greek features intended to present Egyptian religion to a Greek audience – and from cemeteries of the early Greeks. Two unfinished portrait heads of a ruler and queen or Aphrodite were found in the palace area, which would suggest that artists were working within the royal palaces on representations of the rulers, probably for public display. The heads are made out of limestone (Figure 6) and the female image is closest to the portrait type of the deified Arsinoe, but might also be associated with Aphrodite. The hairstyle is unusual in that it is loosely tied at the back of the head rather than neatly wrapped into a bun and there are no royal or divine attributes; there are also no traces of paint, supporting the idea that this unfinished piece was a model.

Figure 7 Greek-style head of Arsinoe II. (Greco-Roman Museum, Alexandria 3262. Photograph by Sally-Ann Ashton.)

As noted, on the coin images of the Theoi Adelphoi, Arsinoe's portrait type is clearly based on that of her brother and it is the posthumous portraits of the deified queen that best illustrate the independent development of the female royal image. It is also possible that some of the portraits, without the usual attributes to distinguish the queen from other royal women, may represent the sister of the rulers, Philoteira, whose cult was celebrated as a separate entity and who must have been represented by, or even associated with, the royal couple. As previously noted, the portraits of Arsinoe II potentially span a much greater period than those of her brother, and most of the available evidence indicates her posthumous image, reflecting the interest and popularity of her cult.

A small head in the Alexandria Museum illustrates one of the portrait types associated with the queen (Figure 7). The portrait has large eyes, thin eyebrows, a straight nose and a clearly

Figure 8 Greek-style head of Arsinoe II. (Musée Royal du Mariemont, Mariemont B.161. Copyright and reproduced with permission of the Musée Royal du Mariemont.)

defined mouth, all of which are softly modelled. The head is slightly raised, with the chin tilted upwards, giving the impression that the queen is gazing past the viewer into the air. Such a position is typically reserved for heroic figures or gods, and for this reason the portrait must represent Arsinoe II as a goddess. A sharper image of the queen, in which she wears a diadem, illustrates the second, possibly contemporary portrait type (Figure 8). The head, which is now in the Mariemont Museum, is believed to have come from Memphis, although, like many other Ptolemaic portraits, the exact find-spot has been lost. This portrait type is still idealised and clearly represents Arsinoe Philadelphos as a deified queen, but the diadem indicates that it is her royal rather than her divine role that is paramount here.

Like Arsinoe II, Berenike II was given her own posthumous cult, in addition to being worshipped along with her husband as the Theoi Euergetai. These forms of deification are explored fur-

Figure 9 Greek-style head of Berenike II from the Sarapieion in Alexandria. (Greco-Roman Museum, Alexandria 3908. Photograph by Sally-Ann Ashton.)

ther in Chapter 6. The proportionately large number of representations of Berenike reflects developments in the ruler cult under Ptolemy IV. However, it is possible that some of the images were intended to represent Arsinoe II but were manufactured during the reign of Ptolemy IV and were influenced by contemporary stylistic developments. The practice of creating posthumous images of the queens potentially causes more confusion with each new succession. Scholars have compared Berenike's portrait type to images of the goddess Aphrodite, while Arsinoe II is likened to images of Artemis by some.

There are two important images of Berenike II from Alexandria. One (Figure 9) was found during excavations in the sanctuary of Sarapis in the southern part of the city. The 'Sarapieion queen' has colour preserved on the hair and eyes. It was found with a bust of the god and has been associated with another male portrait, now in Paris, which is believed to be part of the group because of shared stylistic features. Although the link seems to be correct, the portrait type is not that of Arsinoe III, as has been suggested, and for this reason the group is more likely to represent Berenike II and Ptolemy III. It may be that the group was manufactured during the reign of Ptolemy IV. It is also unlikely that it represents Cleopatra I, which has also been proposed, not least because the main period for royal patronage at the Alexandrian Sarapieion is under Ptolemies III and IV who were responsible for the sanctuary's construction. Thus it would make more sense for the queen's portrait to date to this period and not to a time when the royal court had been moved to Memphis. The diadem rather than *stephane* indicates that, in this group, Berenike II is represented as queen rather than goddess. Sarapis was a Greek version of an already existing Egyptian hybrid deity: Osiris-Apis, in other words the cult of the dead Apis bull, which was based at Memphis where the bulls lived and were subsequently buried. The bulls were revered because they were believed to be the living embodiment of the god Ptah and so in death they were mummified. It was usual for the king to pay for the burial of these creatures, which was a costly affair but

Figure 10 *Greek-style statue of Berenike II and her daughter, princess Berenike from Alexandria. (Greco-Roman Museum, Alexandria 14942. Photograph by Sally-Ann Ashton.)*

one that the Ptolemies continued. In order to present Osiris-Apis to the Greeks, a new Greek-style iconography was adopted and a sanctuary was built in Alexandria during the reigns of Ptolemies I to IV. In late antiquity Clement of Alexandria, quoting Athenaeus, states that the cult statue of Sarapis was made of precious metals and encrusted with jewels; it is likely that the portrait head of Berenike II would have been slotted into a similar body and would have stood with the cult statue of the god. During the Hellenistic period there was a preference for using marble from the Greek island of Paros. Composite statuary was commonly used for cult statues in classical Greek temples, often on a colossal scale and made of precious materials such as ivory.

Another image of Berenike from Alexandria illustrates a different role: that of mother, which may well be associated with the longer standing Egyptian tradition (Figure 10). In a rare full-length statue, Berenike appears with a small child standing at her side. The mother is veiled, probably in mourning and the child looks upward, in a pose associated with apotheosis (deification). This is likely to be the young princess Berenike who died while a child and whose deification is mentioned in the Canopus decree of 238 BC, which was written following a priestly synod. We do not, unfortunately, have an exact find-spot within Alexandria for the representation, but it seems likely that it was placed in either a sanctuary or public place and was intended to be a study of the queen and her child. The overall impression is idealised, with the child, shown disproportionately small, leaning against her mother's knee. The statue is not of the best quality; it was produced from local limestone and the carving is not exceptional but it is nevertheless important because it gives an impression of how the other heads would have looked in their original setting.

There are further provenanced images of Berenike II, from both her lifetime and after her death. At Hermopolis Magna, which lies in the Nile Valley south of the Faiyum, a temple was built by soldiers to Ptolemy II, Arsinoe II, Ptolemy III and Berenike II. The building was Greek Doric in style and the entablature preserves the dedicatory inscription which states that it was dedicated by Greek soldiers in honour of their king; it was probably financed by booty from the third Syrian war (246–241 BC). The temple is one of the few in the area to have been systematically excavated, although only parts of the Ptolemaic sanctuary survive due to the re-use of building materials in later antiquity. Wace, who excavated the site in the 1950s, suggested that the form of the temple was similar to the Ptolemaion or Arsinoeion at Alexandria and that it was a traditional Doric-style building. A statue was retrieved during the excavation, and although no inscription was found and the state of preservation was too fragmentary to allow identification, Wace suggested that the subject was Berenike II. The statue was Greek in style and showed a seated, Aphrodite-type figure with heavy drapery. Another head from the site, and now in the Mariemont Museum, shows a similar portrait type to Berenike's other representations

Figure 11 *Greek-style head of Berenike II from Hermopolis (Musée Royal du Mariemont, Mariemont B.264. Copyright and reproduced with permission of the Musée Royal du Mariemont.)*

(Figure 11). As the upper part of the head is missing its stucco finish, it is not possible to know if it represented a queen or a goddess. It is very similar in style to the head from the Alexandrian Sarapieion.

There are a number of small portrait heads of Berenike II from Alexandria, probably from sanctuaries and dedicated on behalf of, or to, the royal family. The carving of these smaller examples, which are generally 12–13 cm in height, is not as skilled as that on the larger heads, probably because, in the life-size or larger portraits, the official royal workshop would have been involved. The comparatively large number of Berenike heads may be on account of the promotion of the queen's cult by her son, Ptolemy IV, which will also be explained in Chapter 6.

There is an interesting group of Greek-style representations from Tell Timai, in the Egyptian Delta. Several rulers are represented, some more than once, and the heads are generally

Figure 12 *Greek-style head of Berenike II from Tell Timai. (The Egyptian Museum, Cairo JE 39517. Photograph by Sally-Ann Ashton.)*

16–19 cm in height. One example probably represents Arsinoe II. In this statue the queen looks straight upwards; the features are less distinctive than on many of the other portraits and yet the remnants of a veil indicate that the subject was more likely to be royal than a goddess. Such statues probably functioned as cult images in smaller sanctuaries within Alexandria. Certainly the description of a temple built by Philadelphos in honour of his sister (with the magnetically supported image of the queen floating around the inner sanctuary) demonstrates, if nothing else, a vivid imagination on the author's behalf (Pliny, *Natural Histories* XXXIV.42–3). The important factor is that nothing seems to have been too elaborate for the Ptolemaic capital – a consideration again illustrated by the description of the festival procession of Ptolemy II. Some images, however, may well have served a civic function within the royal palaces and public areas of the city as a reminder to the people of their rulers.

Figure 13 (a) Greek-style head of Arsinoe III from Tell Timai;
(The Egyptian Museum, Cairo JE 35334. Photograph by Sally-Ann Ashton.)

Figure 13 (b) Profile, showing the queen's distinctive portrait type. (The Egyptian Museum, Cairo JE 35334. Photograph by Sally-Ann Ashton.)

There are two types of representation of Berenike II – one with the hair pulled back into a bun and the other with corkscrew locks (Figure 12) – showing both the living and the posthumous portrait type of the queen. This is the earliest example of a sculpture with the corkscrew hairstyle in Egypt and it is commonly described as a representation of a queen that is associated with the goddess Isis. There is nothing, however, to indicate that this particular coiffure was associated with the goddess until the Roman period; the Ptolemaic examples are linked to the personification of Libya and also Africa, and adopted by Ptolemaic queens when they appear as deified queens. The style is more commonly found in the second century BC, and were it not for the characteristically prominent chin, this sculpture would fit more comfortably in this period. Of the living type, two examples survive; they are carved by different sculptors but show the same characteristic features. Finally, there is a sterner portrait type from Tell Timai, which is closest to that of Arsinoe III. This head is shown with a diadem, suggesting that she was still alive and shown as queen. A finer portrait of Arsinoe III with an extremely stern expression was found at Bubastis (Figures 13a and 13b). Her hair is rolled upwards in a style also found on her coin portraits, but on the marble head she displays characteristics of her brother's portrait image. In addition to images of the queens – the identity of which is disputed with one scholar identifying the Berenike posthumous image as a representation of Isis – there are portraits of male rulers. Alexander the Great, Ptolemy III as Dionysos, Ptolemy II, Ptolemy IV and a bust of a naked or probably half-draped Aphrodite were also found at Tell Timai and are all housed in the Egyptian Museum in Cairo. The statues probably made up a family group, and the reason for the number of images of Berenike II may well be her promotion by her son. The group ends with a certain representation of Arsinoe III, which would support that it was set up during the reign of Ptolemy IV, who obviously wanted to promote his predecessors and the development of his mother's personal cult.

A small head, now in the Alexandria Museum, also probably represents Arsinoe III. The features are not very clear because of the sculpture's small scale; however, the profile is similar to that of Arsinoe III. It is an important piece, mainly because the veil and stephane were carved from the marble and so survive intact. The head gives an impression of how the many portraits, now without their headdresses, would have appeared. The large eyes, mouth and chin are very similar to the Bubastis head; the distinctive profile and sullen mouth remain the same, but the slight twist of the head results in a less severe image. Portraits of Arsinoe III generally have a stern appearance, with a precisely sculpted nose, that is very close to her coin profiles. The portrait type shows a marked contrast to that of earlier queens; although it is idealised, it offers an insight to the queen's character. The ancient author Athenaeus, in a work entitled *Athenaeus Deipnosophistai* (276 A–C), recounts a story of the queen's emotional plea to her brother to stop the debauched and constant drink parties in the royal palaces. There is a move away from the idealised, divine images that are seen under Arsinoe II and Berenike II; this may reflect the fact that Arsinoe III was not deified in her own right but was worshipped only with Ptolemy IV, as the Theoi Philopatores (father-loving gods).

Some portraits are difficult to identify because they appear to be hybrids of the portraits of Berenike II and Arsinoe III. Overall the images are closer to the known representations of Arsinoe III, but they do not conform to her standard portrait type. They show a mature woman, with the heavy eyelids more commonly found on the portraits of earlier queens; the nose is small and the mouth is finely carved with a slightly sullen appearance. Although some of these features, such as the eyes and nose, are similar to those on the first group of Berenike II's portraits, the overall effect is closer to the images of Arsinoe III.

The reign of Cleopatra I saw the more regular adoption of the corkscrew coiffure by the Ptolemaic royal women, probably because of its established use on Egyptian-style representations. What we see in the capital city, however, is the gradual replacement of purely Greek-style statuary for images that show the royal family as Egyptians, but which have Greek portrait features thus enabling the Greeks to read the image and recognise the ruler. It consists of rows of ringlets, either of one length or with a shorter row lying on top of the longer locks. The queens still wear a diadem or stephane and, on occasion, a veil. Several small-scale portraits survive, and again one must presume that these images were perhaps associated with citizens who wished to make a dedication on behalf of the royal house, compared to the larger scale portraits that are more likely to have been more closely connected with the rulers. This, in conjunction with the poor coin record for the second century BC, would explain why the portrait features are not instantly recognisable and seem to have been intended as a more general type of image with less attention to detail. The existence of the very grand images, as seen from the Sarapieion queen, to the minor ones that would have been affordable by the relatively poor, illustrates the remarkable penetration of the ruler cult into society at all levels.

Many scholars assume that these images were specifically made to represent the queens as Isis, both in Greek- and Egyptian-style statues. However, such conclusions are heavily influenced by our knowledge of the iconography of Isis in the Roman period and there is little to suggest that the link held good in the second century BC. These locks first appear on portraits of Berenike II, showing the queen, of Cyrenaican origin, as a personification of Libya. Although it is perhaps less interesting to conclude that the so-called 'Isis coiffure' was, at the time of its introduction, simply a reflection of a new fashion that was associated with the Ptolemaic queens and was only subsequently adopted to represent Isis (with whom they assimilated themselves), this is the most plausible explanation for its appearance. The fact that there are no surviving portraits in the round of Cleopatras I to V with the melon coiffure would support the idea that the hairstyle was indeed a fashion. The lack of evidence for Cleopatra VII, who is known to have been closely associated with Isis, being portrayed with this coiffure on Greek-style images supports the proposed explanation.

Figure 14 *Greek-style fragment of a bust, probably representing Cleopatra III. (Greco-Roman Museum, Alexandria 3420. Photograph by Sally-Ann Ashton.)*

Of the later queens there is a small Greek-style bust from Alexandria (Figure 14). This portrait type can be associated with Cleopatra III and was found on both Greek and Egyptian-style representations. The head turns sharply upwards and the face is fleshy with a small down-turned mouth. The Venus rings on her neck are clearly visible but the overall appearance of the bust is harsher than the portraits of her predecessors. The artist has attempted to recreate the same sharp, upward movement that is seen on a larger bust which is now in the Louvre Museum, Paris, and is the most striking of this group. It is distinct from the smaller marble heads because it is more carefully manufactured and has the 'hallmarks' of a major royal workshop. Like the Egyptian-style portraits it is masculinising. There are two smaller scale fragments of statues, also housed in the Louvre Museum, which are thought to have come from Hermopolis Magna. The portrait features on the statues are not the same, and the hair is styled differently, but all show the queen wearing a corkscrew coiffure. The most striking resemblance is the dynamic pose,

91

which illustrates that this development was perhaps the result of a single artist's work, which was then copied on smaller scale representations.

Both portraits probably represent Cleopatra III, wife of Ptolemy VIII, who later ruled with her two sons Ptolemies IX and X. It clearly shows a mature subject, and this is accentuated by the sharp movement of the queen's head and her stern expression. It has been suggested that as a type it echoes the increasing power that was enjoyed by the queens and their new role of either regent or ruler in their own right. As there was no iconography available at this time for expressing a queen's political power, the royal women adopted male physical characteristics, often of their consort, in order to promote their status. This is also true of the last Cleopatra's coin portraits. Walker has argued that the later coin portraits of Cleopatra VII, in which she appears very masculine, make her resemble her Roman lover Mark Antony. Both recall the appearance of Cleopatra's father, Ptolemy XII, showing the tradition to be Ptolemaic. A marble head from Cherchel (Algeria) offers a sculpted version of the genre for Cleopatra VII and a second veiled head from the same site may represent her daughter Cleopatra Selene in similar fashion.

No sculptures have been identified as Cleopatra V Tryphaina or Berenike IV. The lack of portraits for the women of this period may reflect the turbulent political situation in Egypt during the first century BC. Unfortunately this lacuna impedes our understanding of the development of these particular queens' images, particularly when the portraits of Cleopatra VII offer a contrast to those of the second-century queens. Her portrait type looks back to the third century BC in both the Greek and Egyptian styles – a move that may have been part of a deliberate policy to reaffirm the dynasty's power.

The queen may have specifically intended to associate herself with Arsinoe II, since she adopts the double cornucopia on the reverse of her coins and quite possibly on statues that are now lost. Her portraits also served to link her with her father in their physical appearance, promoting her as the rightful heir and reflecting her cult title of Philopator or father-loving. Coin images show that the queen was represented with a melon coiffure and royal diadem rather than the corkscrew locks; on the majority of her coins minted in Egypt and Syria, Cleopatra was shown as a ruler and not as a goddess. The exception to this observation are the coins minted in Cyprus to celebrate the birth of Ptolemy Caesarion, where she is shown with a stephane and sceptre and is therefore divine. In Egypt, the same image without the infant appears on the Edfu sealings.

All three of the marble portraits that have been identified as the queen also show her as a royal rather than goddess. On her coins and with regard to these heads Cleopatra disassociated herself from Egypt in that she is shown as a young ruler rather than an Egyptian queen. In the political and international arena Cleopatra was a Greek. In Egypt she was a goddess and ruler of Egypt. The only non-Hellenised portrait of the queen to be found abroad is the marble Greek-style head showing an Egyptian goddess from the Esquiline Hill in Rome (see front cover). As will be noted in Chapter 6, the circumstances of this particular dedication in an Egyptian sanctuary warranted the representation of Cleopatra as Isis. What is fascinating about this head is that it has been adapted for a non-Egyptian audience. Even religion abroad was culturally sensitive, it seems.

Of the three identifiable portraits in the round, the Berlin and the Vatican heads are more Roman than Hellenistic in appearance. The Cherchel portrait was found in Mauretania, modern Algeria, but has more in common with the Alexandrian portraits of the second century BC and with the portraits of Auletes. All three show a youthful image, with strong nose and a rounded face, very similar to the coin portraits from Egypt and many of the seal impressions from Edfu. The finest of the three is the Berlin head; careful attention has been given to such details as curls on the forehead. The piece is clearly a copy of the same portrait type that appears on the Alexandrian coins and yet there is a distinctly Roman treatment of the hair, which might suggest that it was manufactured in Italy rather than imported from Egypt. Similarly, the Vatican Cleopatra offers a slightly poorer version of the same portrait type.

If the pair were manufactured in Italy there is an obvious question concerning their function. It is possible that they were brought over from Egypt for Octavian's triumphal march, or that they were manufactured in Italy as copies of the queen's image. It is also possible that, since one was found at the Villa of Quintilli, which can be dated to the second century AD, they could have been collection items, like the portraits from the villa of the Papyri at Pompeii, which will be discussed further in Chapter 7. Their date is surely still BC and while Octavian is said to have left the gold statue of Cleopatra in the temple of Venus it is unlikely that he would have promoted her beyond the gesture of saving an image that Caesar erected. For this reason it seems unlikely, but not impossible, that other portraits of Cleopatra were manufactured during her stay in Rome. One further possibility is that the statues represent Cleopatra Selene, but the close similarity between the sculptures and the coin portraits of Cleopatra VII would imply that the sculptures were intended to represent the queen and not her daughter.

The same argument could well be used for the Cherchel head, which offers a more stylised version of the same portrait. This particular piece seems to have more in common with Alexandrian portraits of the second century BC; the strong brow and mouth are very similar to some of the smaller marble sculptures from Alexandria. Is it possible for this particular head to have been manufactured in Egypt? To answer this particular question a closer look at the queen's policy in Egypt and the promotion of her image is required. In Egypt Cleopatra was shown as the queen in traditional attire, and it is an interesting fact that there are no recognised Greek portraits of Cleopatra from Egypt in the round. This follows the trends set in the second century BC, when those in the Egyptian tradition replace the Greek-style representations.

Cleopatra VII's retrospective image may be associated with political aspirations as well as a willingness to evoke past ages. The initial use of Greek-style representations present the Ptolemaic royal women as queens and show them offering to gods or accompanying images of the god, in a sort of flirtation with their own divinity. This can be seen clearly in the case of the Sarapieion queen, who wears a diadem but appears on the same scale as the cult statue of Sarapis and as part of the Theoi Euergetai with her husband and consort. The decrease in the Greek-style portraits of the queens coincides with the cessation of the faience cult vases and perhaps represents a broader acculturation. The Greek images are for the most part replaced with Egyptian-style images of the queens as goddesses with an iconography that would be recognisable to all members of the population. Cleopatra VII's revival was aimed at a new audience and her political aspirations meant that she had to look back and perhaps re-learn the 'language' of the Greeks and Romans. That Egyptian statues meant nothing to the latter group is evident from their re-use and, some might say, abuse of the Ptolemaic royal image – a phenomenon that will be explored further in Chapter 7.

CHAPTER 5

Continuing the tradition: queens of Egypt

The initial inspiration for the Ptolemaic female royal image seems to have come from earlier periods of Egyptian artistic representation. The first queen to adopt an earlier but specific form of Egyptian image was not the first of the dynasty, but Arsinoe II, who was wife and sister of Ptolemy II and ruled from *c*. 275 to 270 BC. The new royal pair, Arsinoe II and Ptolemy II, cemented their relationship by presenting themselves as the *Theoi Adelphoi* or sibling gods, and Ptolemy II took the title *Philadelphos* or brother-loving, after the title of his queen. Arsinoe II only ruled in Egypt for five years, and we know of no children from the sibling marriage. Following her death she was deified in her own right, allocated her own cult, temples and priestesses and it was decreed that a statue of the new goddess should be placed in every temple in Egypt. Thus like many of her successors Arsinoe II became a temple-sharing goddess and was cared for in the same manner as any traditional Egyptian deity.

Thus Egyptian artists were charged with the task of distinguishing between Arsinoe II and Arsinoe I, and Arsinoe II in her various roles as goddess, queen and sibling god. In order to do this, artists turned to earlier periods for inspiration, and specifically to occasions when it was necessary to distinguish the chief royal wife from the other wives of the pharaoh. This link is nowhere more apparent than in the adoption of the double uraeus on Egyptian style images of Arsinoe II. The reappearance of the pharaonic royal insignia on the statues of Arsinoe marks an important step in the presentation of the Ptolemaic royal women in Egyptian tradition. The parallel with the use in Greek-style representations of a double horn of plenty on both the statues and coins of Arsinoe II illustrates not only an attempt to promote a coherent policy to Greeks and Egyptians, but also the importance of the presentation of the royal women from an early stage of the dynasty's development. Arsinoe II effectively became ambassador and role model for the royal family, and the continued popularity of her cult into the Roman period is a testimony to the lasting success of her brother's policy of promoting his sister and wife. That artists, possibly under advice from the court advisers, priests or the ruler himself, decided to draw upon an already established attribute raises two important points: firstly, that the Ptolemaic rulers, despite their Macedonian origins, drew from earlier Egyptian traditions and, secondly, that during a period of important developments within the royal cults, a queen played a key role. The dependence on pharaonic example is understood by the re-use of earlier Egyptian sculpture, interestingly from the Amarna period: thus a statue perhaps once representing Nefertiti was re-used or certainly used as a model for an image of an early Cleopatra.

Some modern historians have interpreted Arsinoe's role as evidence of a move towards equality for women, which was then extended to the female populace of Egypt during this time. Such a liberated and surely modernising interpretation is, however, negated by the view that sees the glorification of Arsinoe as little more than exploitation by Ptolemy II in order to promote his own divine status. This is particularly important with regard to the attitude of Greeks in Egypt at this time. For Egyptians, it was acceptable, in fact essential, that their ruler was a god, because without such status accorded to the reigning pharaoh, order or *Ma'at* could not prevail and chaos would rule. For traditional

Greeks, however, it was not acceptable for a mortal to be divine; this same problem was one which Julius Caesar and Mark Antony would encounter in Republican Rome and it was arguably Julius Caesar's divine aspirations, perhaps encouraged by Cleopatra VII, that resulted in his assassination at the hands of fellow Romans. Alexander the Great had been the first Greek to be declared divine, and his early successors promoted him as a god, and by association elevated their own status. Ptolemy II's decision to deify his deceased sister was in many respects simply another means of promoting himself by association, and the divinisation of Arsinoe could be understood as an extension of the situation of the living royal couple, paired as divine. This concept is, in some respects, similar to the association of royal women from the New Kingdom and Third Intermediate period with the god Amun, and it was perhaps no coincidence that Arsinoe was associated with this particular deity in her titles and on two inscribed statues. The fragment of a triad from the island of Pharos in Alexandria shows the royal couple with the god Amun. Ptolemy II sits in the centre protected on one side by Amun and on the other by Arsinoe, who must by this time have been deceased. In the titles Arsinoe is described as daughter of Amun, an association that is found on other posthumous representations of the queen. On other occasions Arsinoe is called daughter of Geb (the creator god), which once again links her to earlier queens. Comprehensive planning is illustrated by the link between the adoption of this title and the crown, which was expressly designed for the queen and which she wore on the many temple relief representations as both one of the sibling gods and as a goddess in her own right. The deified Arsinoe was thus established as a role model for the dynasty. Even in the role of queen, it is difficult to isolate the mortal from the divine because the queens played an important part within the dynastic cult, as noted in the case of Arsinoe II.

Although many of the Ptolemaic queens enjoyed privileges and powers that may be perceived as liberating by the modern historian, the reality could not have been further from the

Figure 15 *Temple relief showing Ptolemy VIII and Cleopatra II or III, Kom Ombo. (Photograph and copyright Sally-Ann Ashton.)*

truth. As queens, the Ptolemaic royal women were the consort of the pharaoh, and while unlike the earlier rulers of Egypt, the Ptolemaic royal men typically took one principal wife, each ruler had courtesans and often children by other women, some of whom obtained a considerable amount of power. The fashion for marrying one's sibling was followed by Ptolemy II and Arsinoe II, Ptolemy IV and Arsinoe III, Ptolemy VI and Cleopatra II, Ptolemy VIII and Cleopatra II, Ptolemy IX and Cleopatra IV, Ptolemy XII and Cleopatra Tryphaina, Ptolemy XIII and Cleopatra VII, and Ptolemy XIV and Cleopatra VII. However, none of these relationships produced consecutive generations of children to brother and sister. These unions also created power struggles in which the queens played a significant part; and indeed the Egyptian temple reliefs offer a unique record of the degree of power held by the royal women, who appear with the pharaoh as illustrated by the representation of Ptolemy VIII and one of his wives at Kom Ombo (Figure 15) and, on occasion, making an offering to the gods alone, as seen on the reliefs showing Cleopatra VII on the bark shrine at Koptos. The inclusion of royal women in offering scenes on Egyptian temples was not universally adopted. The scenes were intended to show the pharaoh in the role of chief priest; only in specific instances was it necessary for the wife of the ruler to appear. Queens could, however, appear as consort to the pharaoh, standing behind him in an offering scene. The exceptions to this rule are Nefertiti, who as previously mentioned was essential to the worship of the Aten, and the royal women who adopted the role of 'god's wife of Amun' also appear alone on temple relief decoration. Rulers, such as queen Hatshepsut, held a different role because she ruled Egypt, and so were expected to adopt the role of pharaoh. In the case of the Ptolemaic royal women, the role of queen was also associated with her divine status in the dynastic cult and so it is often difficult to distinguish a statue or representation showing the queen as consort, from one showing her as part of the dynastic cult. From the time of Arsinoe II, these two roles were intertwined.

It has been suggested that the more traditional Egyptian-style images of the Ptolemaic royal women were used to represent them in their role as queen. These representations show the queens with a clinging, sheath-like dress, sometimes decorated with a broad necklace or pectoral; the hair is covered by a tripartite wig, which consists of two lappets covering the shoulders at the front, and a broader partition of hair at the back. Arms are either held by the sides, clenching a bar (thought to represent a staff or other emblem, or simply act as a space filler), alternatively the queen may hold a sistrum or rattle in the left hand, with the arm drawn across the lower abdomen. The latter category seems to have been particularly associated with representations of queens with the double and triple uraeus. Towards the end of the dynasty, divisions become blurred and representations showing queens in the traditional costume and wig include the cornucopia or horn of plenty that was initially reserved for statues of queens as goddesses in their own right and was associated with the knotted garment and corkscrew wig. This integration is representative of a conscious ideological amalgamation of the two roles.

In the Egyptian tradition Arsinoe II stands apart from her successors in the adoption of a specific iconography, which included the double uraeus and cornucopia, and a crown peculiar to her; some of her images are also inscribed. The similarity between images of the queen in different media within a single culture is illustrated by a comparison between the relief representations and statues in the round; Arsinoe II, for instance, wears the same crown on both. The association of the Greek-style double cornucopia – which was ultimately adopted by the Egyptian artists for images of the queen, but first appears on the reverse of coins and on images of the queen on faience cult vases – must have been intentional, but following Arsinoe II a more general iconography for the entire image was adopted for the royal women.

As queens, the Ptolemaic females wore a crown which consisted of two plumes, a sun-disk and cow's horns, thus associating them with Hathor and Ra. They also wore the uraeus or cobra, normally in a single form, which again represented the eye of Ra and offered protection. This symbol also distinguished the queens from other goddesses who traditionally wore the vulture head, often with the wings placed over the wig, as a mark of divinity.

None of the statues representing queens has a unique prove-nance, with the exception of a portrait of Arsinoe II, which is identified as such because of the double uraeus but remains con-tested by some scholars on account of its find-spot, Kom Abu Billo, in the Egyptian Delta. Stylistically the piece is similar to statues from the 30th Dynasty, a period for which there is evi-dence at the site. This similarity may, however, be further evi-dence of the wish of members of the new dynasty to associate themselves with the last Egyptian pharaohs. No such examples have been found in Alexandria, probably because to the early Greek settlers, such an image would have been unintelligible. By the first century BC, however, purely Egyptian-style images of Ptolemaic queens do appear in the capital, and these will be dis-cussed in the last chapter of this book. Also, from the later Ptolemaic period comes a fragment of an Egyptian-style statue, although only the crown survives. Sir William Mathew Flinders Petrie found the fragment in the temple of Min at Koptos; it is unusual because it is inscribed, and has three uraei. The triple rather than double uraeus has led to the questioning of the orig-inal identification of the subject as Arsinoe II, and it has been suggested that the crown belonged to a statue of Cleopatra VII – a statue dedicated during her co-rule with Ptolemy XIV, with whom she appears on a nearby shrine and with whom she ruled from 47 to 44 BC. The titles on the back of the crown refer to 'king's daughter', 'king's sister' and 'royal wife', thus evoking titles of the past and placing the queen firmly within the boundaries of queenship rather than kingship. It should be noted that not even when ruling with Caesarion, her son, did Cleopatra VII adopt the dress of a male pharaoh. The spread of known find-spots implies that this form of representation was universal in Egypt and prob-ably, at least initially, functioned within the Egyptian temples.

Figure 16 *Egyptian-style statue of Arsinoe II, brought from Egypt to Rome. (Vatican Museums 22681. Photograph copyright and reproduced with permission of the Vatican Museums.)*

Even with a lack of provenance and inscription the statues can be placed in rough order to reveal the development of the Ptolemaic royal image in the Egyptian tradition. A colossal granite inscribed representation of Arsinoe II, now in the Vatican Museums, establishes a chronological sequence for Egyptian-style representations of the queens (Figure 16). The statue not only shows the portrait type of the queen, but also her associated iconographic attributes. The statue is one of a group of two or three, found in the gardens of Sallust in Rome, but originating from Egypt. One of this group is an inscribed statue of Ptolemy II, which would suggest that this pair represents the Theoi Adelphoi. The third is interesting: only the base is Ptolemaic, the rest has been re-cut and joined to the original section which consists of the base and feet of a female statue. The inscription on the back pillar of the statue of Arsinoe reads:

> The princess, inherent; daughter of Geb, the first, the daughter of the bull *mrhw*, the great generosity, the great favour, the daughter of the king, sister and spouse (of the king), woman of Upper and Lower Egypt, image of Isis, beloved of Hathor, mistress of the two lands, Arsinoe, who is beloved to her brother, beloved of Atum, mistress of the two lands.

The titles strongly evoke Egypt's past. We shall return to this group of statues in Chapter 7 in order to consider how they got to Rome, but the imposing pair, or rather triad, illustrates a desire on behalf of the Ptolemaic rulers to show themselves as king and queen of Egypt. The restored statue probably represented a goddess, or was perhaps part of a statue of another queen whose consort is lost.

It should, however, be noted that this particular group of royal representations – that is to say, those that owe their style to the Egyptian tradition – is in fact the smallest. In addition to another unprovenanced example with the double uraeus, now in the Egyptian Museum in Cairo, and a second representation of Arsinoe wearing the double uraeus and her specific crown, there are few that are identifiable. In addition to fragments of heads and bodies (unfortunately not joining) of an idealised and general nature which can probably be dated to the third century BC, there are a couple of small-scale statues which show the subject with a vulture headdress and uraeus and which may date to the second century BC on account of the amalgamation of royal and divine headdress; both are unprovenanced and of a poor quality. One wears the vulture headdress but is without either the vulture or cobra head.

There is, however, one further group of statues that are stylistically very similar in that their features do not follow the idealised model of the images of Arsinoe II. Within this group there is one, now in the Royal Ontario Museum, Toronto, with a single uraeus but the other examples have three cobras on their brow. These images are now housed in the Rosicrucian Museum in San Jose, the Louvre Museum in Paris, and the Egyptian Museum in Turin, with three further examples of a statue representing a deified queen in St Petersburg, the Metropolitan Museum of Art in New York, and the Brooklyn Museum of Art. Scholars do not agree on the identity of this important group of statues and the meaning of the triple uraeus is problematic. The earliest discussion of the triple uraeus dates to the early 1960s, when two leading Late period scholars, Bothmer and Müller, considered the date and meaning of the three cobras in relation to a statue of a deified Ptolemaic queen. Bothmer suggested that the three cobras represented three rulers and so the most likely candidate to wear the motif was Cleopatra II, who had ruled as part of two triads: with her brothers and with her brother and daughter. A brief consideration of the turbulent years surrounding this particular queen is enough to cast doubt on this hypothesis and there are stylistic reasons for linking these images with the last Cleopatra. Müller, on the other hand, concluded that there was no such thing as a triple uraeus and that the third cobra simply represented a vulture head and was by this date stylised. This hypothesis would work for the Turin queen because she wears a vulture headdress over her wig; none of the other statues, however, wears a vulture headdress. Various scholars have made reference to individual statues within this group, which, as noted, also includes images of deified queens. Some tentatively dated the group to the first century BC, suggesting that the subject might be Cleopatra VII. However, scholars have shied away from identifying images of this queen because of her fame. Everybody wants to know what the last Cleopatra looked like and to associate her with any image causes nothing less than a public and media sensation. During the preparation for a recent special exhibition on Cleopatra VII, however, it was suggested that the triple uraeus could be linked to the last Ptolemaic queen. The reasons for this association were the consistency of stylistic features on the statues, and the discovery of a previously unrecognised gem showing a Greek-style image of a diademed woman with Cleopatra's features with a triple uraeus above her head. Moreover, one of the statues holds a double cornucopia, a symbol only associated with Arsinoe II and Cleopatra VII.

The faces of the statues were not what the media had hoped for. Here, rather than a starlet was a mature woman with a prominent chin and a severe mouth that gave a rather sullen appearance. Like the images of the earlier Cleopatras, these representations were identical to those of first-century BC male rulers, which supported the idea that the statues represented Cleopatra VII rather than Cleopatras II or III. In this way the queens were able to link themselves visually with their consorts. If the Koptos crown also represented Cleopatra VII, then the queen adopted the three cobras while still married to her younger brother Ptolemy XIV. As noted, the pair appear on the walls of a bark shrine at the site, and the queen is referred to as 'royal wife' on the back pillar. But what of the statue with a single uraeus, now in the Royal Ontario Museum? Stylistically this piece shares features with those decorated with a triple uraeus. The sculptor has attempted to recreate the rounded, soft features that appeared on earlier statues, but like those with three cobras, the result has a harder, more mechanical appearance. It has to be remembered that Cleopatra VII ruled with her father,

Figure 17 Temple relief showing Ptolemy II, Isis and Arsinoe II, Philae. (Photograph and copyright Sally-Ann Ashton.)

Figure 18 Gateway relief showing Ptolemy III and the Theoi Adelphoi (sibling gods), Karnak. (Photograph and copyright Sally-Ann Ashton.)

by herself and also with her brother Ptolemy XIII and Caesarion; and this may therefore be an image from her early days as queen.

It is not only statues in the round that illustrate the promotion of Ptolemaic queens in the Egyptian tradition. Queens also appear on the relief decorations of temple walls and on official stelae both in a royal and a divine role. Arsinoe II provides an early example of this: at the temple of Isis at Philae where Arsinoe stands behind Isis and receives an offering from Ptolemy II (Figure 17), and on the gateway of Ptolemy III, which was in actual fact completed by Ptolemy IV, where Ptolemy III is shown making an offering to his 'parents' the sibling gods (Figure 18). On the Mendes stela, however, Arsinoe appears twice, once as queen standing behind her consort and then as a goddess receiving the offering from the king. As queen, she performs a ritual task, shaking *sistra* (rattles) in front of the gods; it should, however, be remembered that by the time the stela was carved she was dead and the very fact that she appears as a goddess receiving offerings leaves no doubt as to her status. The fact that she performs such a task as queen is, however, important in itself. A double appearance was not common, but was acceptable in Egyptian representations which were meant to be read as if a language; importance was indicated by placement and the relief effectively became a narrative. If the royal couple or queen was divine then what better way of promoting their status on an official document? We shall return in Chapter 6 to the part played by queens in the royal cults. The crucial question here with regard to their role as ruler of Egypt is whether they adopted (what was essentially) the role of the pharaoh, who as chief priest tended to the needs of the gods. In practice, this was impossible and so priests performed the daily rituals necessary for the care of the god in their charge. This involved washing, feeding and sometimes accompanying the statue of a god on a journey to another temple. For Egyptians, the small cult statues housed in temples represented the god's presence and he or she was cared for accordingly.

From the time of Ptolemy II the queens regularly appear with their consorts in acts of offering to the gods. This phenomenon

THE LAST QUEENS OF EGYPT

was exceptional in earlier dynastic practice. As noted in Chapter 1, Nefertiti directly worshipped the Aten both alongside Akhenaten and alone; other New Kingdom queens would, on occasion, accompany the pharaoh in an offering scene. Royal women who fulfilled the position of 'god's wife of Amun' were also elevated to a status where they would appear alone on temple reliefs, because their ritualistic role necessitated this. The titles adopted by the Ptolemaic queens are quite informative to any understanding of their roles and status and will be considered shortly. It is revealing that queens regularly appear with their consorts in offering scenes: for example, Berenike II was shown alongside her husband, both offering and receiving from the gods. Also on the temple of Opet at Karnak the same queen wears the ceremonial dress of a male ruler, as she accompanies her husband on the upper register of the platform.

There was a development, however, within the dynastic cults, which should be considered outside the role of the rulers as gods. In 105/4 BC Cleopatra III became the priestess of Alexander in Alexandria, as illustrated by the first part of this document:

> In the reign of Cleopatra, Thea Euergetis, also called Philometor, Dikaiosyne, Nikephoros and of Ptolemy Alexander, in the 13=10th year, while queen Cleopatra Thea Euergetis, also called Philometor, Dikaiosyne, Nikephoros was serving as priestess of the cult of Alexander, and of the Theoi Soteres, Theoi Adelphoi, Theoi Euergetai, Theoi Philopatores and of the Theoi Epiphaneis and of the Theos Eupator and of the Theos Philometor and of the Theos Neos Philopator and of the Theos Euergetes, and of the Theoi Philometores ...
>
> [continued in Chapter 6]

In this role Cleopatra III moved closer to the role of pharaoh, a remarkable step as the priesthood of Alexander had been hitherto reserved for males. Cleopatra III's son, Ptolemy IX, was also named as priest of the cult of Alexander; unfortunately the names are removed from the dating formulae after this point and so we do not know if Berenike IV also adopted this role. Arsinoe II had already been the priestess of the ram from Mendes, but this was a local cult. As queen of Ptolemy VIII, Cleopatra III had appeared alternatively with her mother on the walls of temples at Kom Ombo and Medinat Habu; on some occasions the three were shown together. This is also true of stelae, where the two queens stand behind their husband. Later, Cleopatra III takes the dominant position and role of pharaoh on the walls of the temple of Khonsu at Karnak and at Deir el-Medina, with her son Ptolemy IX standing behind her. At the temple of Horus at Edfu the ruler is not shown independent of Horus, because in Egyptian theology he was Horus. Cleopatra III, however, also appears, standing alone shaking *sistra*; in the accompanying texts she is described as 'mother of the gods'.

During her co-rule with Ptolemy IX, Cleopatra III shows a greater than usual autonomy in that she appears in front of her son or makes offerings alone at the rebuilt temple of Nekhbet-Hathor at el-Kab, and she is named in the inner hall of the temple of Isis at el-Hella. Such independence was also displayed by Cleopatra VII, on the Bark shrine of Geb, at the temple of Min at Koptos. The queen and her consort appear individually, as equals, offering to the gods. It has been suggested that the shrine dates to the queen's reign with Ptolemy XIV rather than her first husband; however, a difficulty with titles of the late Ptolemies is that they took the same names and it is therefore difficult to distinguish between Ptolemies XII, XIII and XIV. Irrespective of the identity of her co-ruler, this form of independence was uncommon even during the Ptolemaic period and illustrates true emancipation for the queens. But even Cleopatra VII was not always represented as emancipated: at Denderah she fulfils a ritual role, accompanied by her son who stands in front of her, the queen shaking a Hathor-form sistrum. The appearance of mother and son on the prominent south wall of the temple promotes his place as consort and pharaoh of Egypt, and advertises their strong bond.

Throughout their rule Ptolemaic queens were given traditional Egyptian titles. Unusually for a book on earlier queens, Troy includes the titles of the queens of the last dynasty; the examples discussed here come from Gauthier, Porter and Moss and Troy, with additional references found during a study of Ptolemaic royal sculpture by the present author. A closer inspection of the types of titles shows that there was both continuation and innovation and that the priesthood allocated titles for which we have no earlier evidence. It is also possible to track links between Ptolemaic queens and those from earlier dynasties. The titles 'lady of all that circles the sun-disk', 'governess' and 'mistress of appearances' were used by earlier 'god's wives' and by Arsinoe II.

Berenike I appears only once in the texts of the temple of Khonsu at Karnak and is called 'mother of the god'. Arsinoe I, the first wife of Ptolemy II, adopts the following titles on a statue from Koptos, now in the Cairo museum: 'sweet of love', 'pleasing appearance', 'the one who fills the palace with beauty', 'the one who brings peace to the heart of Upper and Lower Egypt', 'great of praises', 'great wife of the king', 'the first great wife of the king of Upper and Lower Egypt', 'lady of the two lands' and 'noblewoman'.

Arsinoe II was posthumously allocated a Horus name and birth name (which were usually the names allocated to the pharaoh), but Berenike II was given full kingly titles during her lifetime. Hölbl notes that in Demotic dating formulae Berenike was called 'the pharaoh (with the feminine "t" at the end of the word) Berenike', thus illustrating her status as a female pharaoh rather than queen and consort. This accords with her appearance on temples receiving from the gods and accompanying her consort. On the temple of Khonsu at Karnak, Berenike II is called the 'ruler', thus directly linking her to the role of pharaoh. This title was also taken by Arsinoe III at the temple of Horus at Edfu, Cleopatra I in the Philae decree, Cleopatra III and Cleopatra V at the Edfu temple, Berenike III and Cleopatra VII at the temple of Montu at Armant and by either Cleopatra V or Cleopatra VII at Kom Ombo (Troy allocates this use to Cleopatra VI).

Berenike II is also called the 'female Horus' in the Philae and Canopus decrees and at the temple of Khonsu at Karnak. Cleopatra I adopts this title at the Edfu temple, Cleopatra III at the Philae temple and Cleopatra VII at the temple of Montu, Armant. Perhaps the most powerful title that was in fact adopted by Arsinoe II, Arsinoe III, Berenike II, Cleopatra I, Cleopatra V, Berenike III and Cleopatra VII: that of the female 'ruler'. These titles are important for our understanding of the developing role of the royal women because they indicate that, in addition to being deified and worshipped, they were promoted to the office of Pharaoh.

Queens were associated with gods in their titulary: Arsinoe II and Cleopatra VII with Geb, the creator god; Arsinoe II, Arsinoe III and Cleopatras I, II, III, IV and V with Re, as either 'daughter of Re' or 'sister-wife of the sun god Re'. Interestingly, however, Arsinoe II is described as 'divine mother', which accords with her adoption by Ptolemy III as his mother. Berenike II is described as 'daughter of the ruler' in the Canopus decree, when in fact she was daughter of a ruler, but not the Egyptian ruler. Traditional titles such as 'king's daughter', 'king's sister' and 'royal wife' are maintained, as are titles connecting the queens to the 'Two Lands'. The titles allowed queens to associate with earlier members of their dynasty, and so many of the newly allocated titles of Arsinoe II reappeared during the reigns of subsequent queens, most especially Cleopatra VII.

What the statues, stelae, temples and titles show is an unequivocal support for the Egyptian tradition, and a willingness by the Egyptian priests to adapt representations and titles to fit the new regime. From the time of Cleopatra I, we see Egyptian-style representation replacing the Greek and we also see recognition of a more powerful role for the Ptolemaic royal women, both politically and within the native Egyptian religion. It is of considerable interest that a statue from the Amarna period should be re-inscribed and re-used as an image of a Ptolemaic queen, because the roles played by the women from these two families had much closer ideological bonds than perhaps any other dynasties.

It is also probably no coincidence that the later, more powerful and independent queens sought to present themselves as Egyptian rather than Hellenistic Greek monarchs, because Egypt had already proved itself able to accept a female pharaoh and the religion allowed a greater autonomy than did the Greek tradition. There may also be a political motive behind the promotion of their Egyptian persona. The native priests were effectively the Egyptian élite and in Thebes they proved to be a powerful force, and one which the Ptolemaic royal family courted by financing building programmes, thus financing the temples and their guardians, the priests. It is ironic, but perhaps telling, that the most prolific periods of temple building occurred during the troubled years of Ptolemies VIII to X which, of course, included Cleopatras II and III.

CHAPTER 6

The royal cults: deification and amalgamation

With new rulers from a foreign culture came innovations in the presentation of the Egyptian royal family, and within this sphere the women played an important and leading role. Within the Greek tradition these developments included the association of the queens with an established deity, which is manifested in inscriptions where, for instance, the goddess, or goddesses, Arsinoe Aphrodite, are invoked; then there is the dynastic cult, in which Arsinoe appeared as a sibling god alongside her brother Ptolemy II. Finally, the queens were deified in their own right, initially posthumously but later in the dynasty, as we shall see, queens were worshipped as goddesses during their lifetime. In this latter capacity the queens became temple-sharing goddesses – in other words, their statue would be placed in every temple in Egypt and they would effectively lodge in the temple of that god.

Association with an existing deity

The association of the Ptolemaic royal house with individual deities is expressed directly by the queens adopting the name of a goddess, which occurs in three different forms. In the first instance the ruler borrows the name of a deity as a cult title. In the second, the queen adds her own name to that of a god or goddess. The final form occurs when a queen refers to herself as the deity, such as Isis or Nea (new) Isis. There is both visual and textual evidence for assimilation to or association with a specific deity in cult titles, inscriptions and representations. In some instances, particularly with Greek culture, the queen simply borrowed the attributes of a specific deity to promote associated qualities rather than assimilate herself with the god. The royal images are therefore an important source for the understanding of this association between deified ruler and the Greek and Egyptian pantheons.

The first goddesses with whom the queens were associated were Greek, as illustrated by the inscriptions on the faience cult vases, previously mentioned in Chapter 4. On the cult vase of Arsinoe II, now in the British Museum (Figure 5, p. 72), the inscription reads 'Agathe Tyche Arsinoe Philadelphos'. These titles therefore suggest that the libation is poured on behalf of the goddess Agathe Tyche and Arsinoe Philadelphos, although the queen herself pours the offering (she is identified by the double cornucopia in her arm). On some of the Arsinoe's altars the name of the goddess Isis appears and Berenike II was associated with the Greek goddess Aphrodite, and also her Egyptian equivalent Isis, during her lifetime. It is likely, therefore, that here the queens were associated with the established goddess of fortune and pour a libation to the goddess Isis. This early association with established divinities shows the queen in a specific role, acting on behalf of the goddess with whom she is associated. Thompson, in her 1972 book on the cult vases, suggests that Tyche's name appears as a sort of personal deity to the queen, which would also make sense of the image, which shows Arsinoe wearing a diadem, and thus being a queen rather than a goddess in her own right. That Isis appears on some fragments of vases shows an early and important reference to the Egyptian goddess and her presentation to the Greeks. This association would be promoted further under the Cleopatras.

This connection with a goddess is equivalent to the ruler Ptolemy III's association with Poseidon, Amun and Helios on his coin portraits. It was not until after her death, however, that Berenike II became a fully-fledged goddess. It was during the reigns of Arsinoe II and Berenike II that the association between queen and Isis is firmly cemented. Isis was promoted to the Greeks from the third century BC, when a small sanctuary was established at the site of the Sarapieion in Alexandria, and of course in the Egyptian tradition the queens were already associated with this particular deity. Isis, as mother of Horus, was a natural choice for a divinity with which the queens could be linked, and we have seen how the iconography for this divine pair was adopted from representations of Old and Middle Kingdom queens with their sons.

Fraser, in his publication of *Ptolemaic Alexandria*, notes that the epithets of Arsinoe following her death do not include the title Philadelphos, which would link her to the ruler cult. Instead streets that are named after her include the name of an existing goddess: Basileia (queen) for Hera, Eleemon for Aphrodite, Teleia for Hera, Chalkiokos for Athena in Sparta; and Thompson refers to street names found in Roman papyri: Karpophoros for Demeter, Nike, Sozousa for Isis and Eleusinia for Demeter. In these names Arsinoe II serves a function for the goddess and presumably the associated cult. Because Arsinoe was deceased, and so a goddess in her own right, these additional associations with existing deities indicate that such a promotion was not only a means of introducing the idea of divine monarchy to the Greeks, but that these links served another purpose in their own right. In the *Lock of Berenike* by the poet Theocritus, Arsinoe Aphrodite is invoked by Berenike II, thus illustrating another example of a deified queen being linked to an existing god. As previously noted in Chapter 4, it is possible that these associations were intended to indicate the guise in which the ruler-god was invoked and thus the specific function they served. This is similar to the later affiliation of Isis to established Roman goddesses in order to supplicate a particular part of the goddess.

Berenike II was also associated with the personification of goddesses both in Libya as Libya and in Egypt as Alexandria, as illustrated by a mosaic from Tell Timai in the Delta (Figure 19).

Figure 19 *Mosaic showing a personification of Alexandria, from Tell Timai. (Greco-Roman Museum, Alexandria. Photograph by Sally-Ann Ashton.)*

The queen is identified by her portrait features but wears a headdress that consists of a ship's prow with her brooch as an anchor. This powerful image which would have once decorated the central section of a floor, perhaps in a public building, is a match for the sea-faring links of Ptolemy III and Poseidon on his coins. Once again, we see the queen linked to a goddess in that she is associated with the specific role of an established deity. The fact that this form of presentation is exclusively Greek is probably no accident, but rather a gentle means of associating the rulers with the divine – a concept that did not have a tradition in Greek religion, with exception of heroes such as Herakles who were made divine. Interestingly, the Ptolemaic rulers believed themselves to be descended from Herakles and the men are sometimes depicted holding the god's club and wearing a lion's skin headdress.

Although her famous namesake may be better known as a living personification of Isis, Cleopatra III was in fact the first

118

queen to be assimilated directly with the goddess, effectively becoming the living embodiment of Isis, mother of the pharaoh who, as noted previously, in Egyptian theology was believed to be the living embodiment of Horus. And so, for the first time a Ptolemaic queen directly replicated a role that had been reserved for the pharaoh, the only difference being that an appropriate goddess had been selected for association.

Cleopatra VII was a goddess from the start of her reign. A stela, now in the Louvre in Paris, states that the object was dedicated on behalf of Cleopatra, goddess and father-loving. The choice of associating herself with her father was certainly deliberate, and is illustrated not only by her adoption of his portrait type on coins but also by her use of the title Nea or New Isis. Ptolemy XII had declared himself to be the New Dionysos; the use of the epithet Nea seems to have been used to stress the fact that these rulers were not only associating with the deity, but had become the god. The idea is one that was not alien to Egyptian culture at least. At Memphis the Apis bulls were believed to be the living embodiment of the god Ptah, just as the living pharaoh was Horus and the dead pharaoh was Osiris. In Cleopatra's case there was no better goddess with whom she could be associated, particularly following the birth of her son by Julius Caesar and the Roman's subsequent death. Cleopatra had effectively become Isis; the father of the pharaoh was dead, murdered, and the only blip in the myth was that Caesar had not been pharaoh and thus in death was not Osiris. Thus the role of single mother suited Cleopatra well.

The only hint of her Egyptian ancestry in Rome was the marble head in Greek-style showing the queen as an Egyptian goddess, and the probable location of this portrait in a sanctuary of Isis and Sarapis would have been appropriate even in Rome. As noted in Chapter 4, her image in Italy shows a young Greek royal, wearing a broad diadem of royalty. The only exception was the statue that Julius Caesar is said to have placed in the temple of Venus Genetrix at Rome, which showed the queen as the goddess. Whether the link between the two personas was made retrospectively is impossible to know. Ancient writers clearly state that the Roman ruler dedicated a gold statue of the queen.

Even following the start of her relationship with Mark Antony, with whom she had three more children, she fulfilled her role as Isis in Egypt at least, and was represented with her son, as seen on the coins minted at Cyprus to celebrate Caesarion's birth. As on all coins, the queen appears with Greek-style attributes, in this case a stephane or crown, indicating her divine rather than royal status; but at the bottom right-hand corner of the coin a small head appears. Thus the coins show mother and child, Isis and Horus or Harpocrates (as the young Horus was often called). Perhaps the most powerful image comes from the fragments on a dyad or double statue, which was found in the Hadra quarter of Alexandria and which is now divided between the museums in Alexandria and Mariemont (Figure 20).

The Hadra queen is important for two reasons: firstly because it illustrates the full amalgamation of queen/goddess and Isis; and, secondly, because of its find-spot. Stylistically the statue is very close to early Ptolemaic representations and was it not for the accompanying male statue, the piece could be dated to the third century BC. Scholars are more or less unanimous in the identification of the female representation: Cleopatra VII. This is not, however, simply a representation of the queen as she appears on the temple reliefs, because on the Hadra statue the subject is no longer a queen but a fully-fledged goddess. She wears a vulture cap and head, thus making her a goddess. She stands with her son, and the two hold hands showing their close bond and the goddesses' support for the pharaoh. Here Cleopatra is Isis fulfilling the protective role, and accompanying her son in a direct parallel to the coins minted to commemorate his birth. What is perhaps of further interest is the description of the site by a nineteenth-century traveller Wilkinson. The statues were found at the site of a sanctuary, which consisted, according to Wilkinson's description, of Greek tholoi (round temples), Egyptian sphinxes and a 'large edifice'. We know from the

Figure 20 *Fragment of an Egyptian-style dyad showing Cleopatra VII as Isis, from Alexandria. (Musée Royal du Mariemont, Mariemont B505. Copyright and reproduced with permission of the Musée Royal du Mariemont.)*

ancient literary sources that Cleopatra's mausoleum was attached appropriately to a sanctuary of Isis; could this be the site of that sanctuary and Cleopatra's mausoleum? Further investigations at the site are necessary, but, given the position of the find-spot, which was in an area known to house earlier burial sites and one which by the first century BC would have been close to the expanding royal palaces, it is a tempting speculation to make.

As mentioned in Chapters 4 and 5, Cleopatra VII presented herself as a Greek outside her native country. There is, however, one exception to this policy: the marble Egyptianising head now housed in the Capitoline Museums, Rome (see front cover). The head is one of the earliest examples of Egyptianising sculpture in Rome and was found in an area of the city where there were late Republican temples to Isis and Sarapis. The portrait type shows a youthful female and is similar to the two Rome Cleopatras now in the Vatican City and Berlin. The difference with the Capitoline head is that although it is carved in marble, and is effectively a bust that was intended to be slotted into a separate body, as was commonly the practice of Hellenistic Greek sculptors, the attributes are Egyptian. Here we see a Greek version of the Hadra goddess, which was possibly even carved by an Egyptian sculptor. The goddess wears a tripartite echeloned Egyptian wig with an extraordinary vulture draped over the top; a crown probably of sun-disk and cow's horns was slotted into the top of the head and the head of the vulture, probably in gold, would have adorned the front of the wig. The piece obviously represents the goddess Isis, and can be linked to Cleopatra VII not only by its stylistic features but also by her policy of presenting herself as Isis. Here, there have been minor changes to make the image comprehensible to the Romans. This statue would complement that in the temple of Venus Gentrix in the Forum of Julius Caesar, where the Roman dedicated a statue of Cleopatra as Aphrodite, perhaps holding the infant Eros, and one again associating Cleopatra and her son with the divine. Unfortunately no traces survive.

The dynastic cult

The development of the cult and any subsequent changes that were made are classified in the dating formulae of decrees and documents from the period, which included the names of the eponymous priests and priestesses. Priests were of Greek origin, and indeed the idea of augmenting the cult of Alexander and the subsequent Ptolemies was essentially a Greek affair. Many of the concepts, however, fitted comfortably within the Egyptian tradition and earlier Egyptian kings had had their own personal cults. What we see then, in the case of the dynastic cult, was a perfect synthesis of two very different beliefs. Alexander had paved the way for deification of a ruler and it was on his foundations that the Ptolemies built. The success in both Greek and Egyptian contexts has survived in considerable quantities. The archaeological evidence for the promotion of the dynastic cult is much greater in Egyptian temples than in Greek sanctuaries, largely because of the native tradition of decorating temple walls with representations of rulers and deities. Before looking more closely at the evidence, however, it is probably worth at this point considering a brief history of the development of rulers as divine beings.

Ptolemy I initiated a cult of Alexander the Great, which was centred on the tomb in Alexandria. Alexander had asked to be buried at Siwa, an oasis in the western desert, where he had been proclaimed son of Amun, the Egyptian equivalent of Zeus. His successors, however, decided that the body should be laid to rest in his country of origin, Macedonia, but as the funeral cortege made its way from Babylon to Macedonia, Ptolemy effectively hi-jacked the body and laid it to rest temporarily at Memphis, until a tomb and sanctuary could be built at Alexandria. Ptolemy II added the cult of himself and Arsinoe II as the Theoi Adelphoi to Alexander's cult in 272/1 BC while Arsinoe, his sister and queen, was still alive. Thus from the beginning, the dynastic cult involved the promotion and worship of living rulers. Following her death in 270 BC, Arsinoe II was then awarded an individual cult, which was allocated separate priestesses called the

Kanephoroi. Hence, from the time of Philadelphos, there was the original cult of Alexander to which the cult of the Theoi Adelphoi was attached and then the cult of Arsinoe II. Ptolemy II also instigated a cult of the Theoi Soteres, but this remained separate from the cult of Alexander and the Theoi Adelphoi until the time of Ptolemy IV. A temple was set up to the founders of the dynasty, probably shortly after the inauguration of their worship, and there are references to the individual worship of the royal pair. As part of his reforms, Ptolemy IV rebuilt the tomb of Alexander to house his ancestors and subsequent rulers, interestingly with a pyramidal form on top of the tomb and sanctuary; he also added the cult of the founders of the dynasty to the main branch of royal cults, and set up an eponymous priesthood in Ptolemais, in Upper Egypt. Ptolemy IV also deified his mother, Berenike II, and as part of his reforms of the royal cults he placed her priestess (Athlophoros) before that of Arsinoe II in the dating formula. The Theoi Euergetai had, of course, joined themselves to the cult of Alexander, the Theoi Adelphoi, and Arsinoe II during their reign.

The late association of the Theoi Soteres with the main cult may explain the general lack of representations of this particular royal couple. It is, however, interesting to note that one of the few images of Ptolemy I and Berenike I to appear in a medium other than coinage, was re-cut in antiquity. Some scholars have suggested that the reason for the original split between cults was that Ptolemy I did not feel that it was appropriate to be associated with his contemporary in order to avoid obscuring the cult of Alexander. There is a similar lack of evidence for images of Alexander the Great and it is not clear whether the Egyptian priesthood accepted the ruler cult of Alexander; there is certainly little evidence for it, which would suggest that promotion by the priests may well have required financial incentives. Therefore, when the ruler either commissioned or added to a temple their image would appear on the walls. It is probably partly for this reason that we have more visual evidence for the royal cults from Egyptian contexts rather than Greek.

The dynastic cult seems to have been an extension of the role played by current rulers as consorts. In terms of Egyptian theology the royal pair was seen to be divine, and so it was no great leap when the idea of divine pairs was introduced to the native priesthood. For the Greeks, however, the idea of a divine living being was not an established belief. Alexander the Great had flirted with divine status, calling himself the son of Amun, but it was only really after his death that cults were established. It was for this reason that Ptolemy I and Berenike I were not deified during their lifetime, preferring instead to promote Alexander and themselves by association. The living Theoi Adelphoi could probably have been justified to the Greeks by the new pharaonic role, but it is perhaps no coincidence that Ptolemy II promoted himself further by enhancing the cult of his dead sister, the logic being that they had been linked in life and now Arsinoe was accepted into both the Greek and Egyptian pantheons as a goddess in her own right receiving offerings, as any other god.

The dynastic cult may have been used as a means of cementing family marriages but Cleopatra I, the wife of Ptolemy V, was a Syrian princess. However, as soon as she married Ptolemy V, in the winter of 194/3 BC, she became part of the dynastic cult of the Theoi Epiphaneis. Following her death – she was murdered by members of the Ptolemaic court – her son established a separate priesthood for her individual cult and also took the title Philometor or mother-loving. It was not, however, long before the Ptolemaic queens were awarded such status during their lifetimes, at their own initiative.

Cleopatra II, sister and wife of Ptolemy VI, also took the title Philometor as half of the Theoi Philometores, until the death of her husband, when she married the younger brother Ptolemy VIII and together they became the Theoi Euergetai – the second rulers to hold this title. As part of the dynastic cult, Cleopatra II was awarded the title Thea Euergetis, or the goddess Euergetis. Cleopatra II, however, ruled Egypt in her own right following the marriage of her brother/husband to her daughter and his niece, Cleopatra III, during a subsequent falling out between the three co-rulers. During this particular period she adopted a new cult title calling herself Thea Philometor Soteira. This new title reflected her link to her first husband and older brother and also her new position as ruler; she also removed the eponymous priesthood for the cult of the Theoi Euergetai from the dating formulae. However, the period of sole rule was short-lived and the Theoi Euergetai returned. This account, however, illustrates the political as well as the religious importance of individual cults.

Under Ptolemy VIII, the ruler and his two queens appear as the Theoi Euergetai, predominantly in Egyptian contexts – the two Cleopatras distinguished by the titles sister and wife respectively. During this time, however, the rulers also assumed the role of priests of the dynastic cult, including Cleopatra III after the death of Ptolemy VIII; the presence of Cleopatra III in a male priesthood is testimony to her independent role as ruler of Egypt. Some scholars have suggested that this development was influenced by the Greek tradition, but there is no precedent for this action. Egyptian rulers, on the other hand, fulfilled the role of priest to the gods and it would seem likely by this period that the role was part of the Egyptian tradition, particularly given the pre-Ptolemaic role of the wives of Amun and their close association with the god. The sons of Cleopatra III also fulfilled the role of priests of the dynastic cult. The complexities of the dynastic cult by the end of the second century BC are illustrated in a Greek document dating to 105/4 BC, during the reign of Cleopatra III, when the queen adopted her own cult titles as illustrated in the latter part of this document, continued from Chapter 5:

> ... when Theodoros son of Seleukos, ... and Exegetes, was priest for life, of queen Cleopatra Thea Euergetis, also called Philometor, Dikaiosyne, Nikophoros; when Mnemosyne daughter of Nikanor was priestess of queen Cleopatra, Thea Euergetis, also Philometor, Dikaiosyne, Nikophoros; when Demetrios son of Theodoros was Hieros Polos of Isis, great mother of gods; when

Olympias, daughter of Seleukos was priestess of Arsinoe Philopator. . . .

In terms of the archaeological record, we see a visual equivalent to the names of priests and their cults. Ptolemy II followed a carefully orchestrated policy of association with his parents and with his sister. His prominence over that of Arsinoe can be seen clearly on the coins minted in honour of the Theoi Soteres and the Theoi Adelphoi; images which leave no doubt as to his intended self-promotion. Egyptian parallels to the coin images can be found on temple reliefs and in the form of statues. The aforementioned Vatican pair of colossal statues, which were found in the gardens of Sallust in Rome, represent the sibling gods Arsinoe II and Ptolemy II (Figure 16, p. 104). And the royal couple are seen as Egyptian gods on the gateway of Ptolemy III at the Karnak temple (Figure 18, p. 108). The new ruler makes an offering to the royal couple, who are awarded a status equal to any more-established Egyptian god. Like the coins it is possible to see how this image worked well in terms of propaganda for the new king, but equally for the priests who would be funded by the royal house and in some cases directly from taxes given by the king. In Greek temples the rulers were worshipped as gods, as illustrated by the temple to the royals at Hermopolis Magna. Worshipping one's ruler had a very obvious advantage in that knowing the object of your patronage was only a letter away, greatly increased the chances of some of the more materialistic requests for divine intervention. Temples like that at Hermopolis and also within Alexandria were quite distinct from those of the deified queens.

It is interesting that, as the third century BC progresses, the queens gain a greater autonomy and the rulers put more effort into promoting themselves with divine regalia rather than by association with other family members. In terms of the images of dynastic pairs, the queens were used and, by the reign of Ptolemy IV, promptly dumped because they no longer served the purpose of being a means of divine association. However, their status was not demoted; on the contrary, they received a greater autonomy. Family feuds and dynastic rivalry may well have been the ultimate reason for liberation, because the queens followed the example of their consorts and were seen to be living goddesses in their own right.

That is not to say that there are no images of divine couples following the death of Arsinoe III. Ptolemy VIII and his wives appear on both temple reliefs, stelae and sealings as previously mentioned, and for political reasons, if nothing else, it was important for the royal family to at least show a united front, even if the reality could have been nothing further from the truth. The golden age for the dynastic cult was without doubt the third century BC, when rulers were experimenting with their divine status.

Goddess

We are fortunate in that both textual and archaeological evidence for the deification and promotion of the cults of Ptolemaic queens survives. The deification of the queen is an important concept in the apotheosis of individuals and is presented nowhere more visually than on the coinage of the period.

On coins minted by Ptolemy II and Ptolemy III, and even as late as the reign of Ptolemy VIII, Arsinoe appears as a goddess wearing a *stephane* (divine crown) and with a sceptre. On the reverse of Arsinoe's coins a double *cornucopia* (horn of plenty) is shown – a motif that also appeared on her statues and on the faience *oinochoai* (jugs), which will be discussed below. Arsinoe III, like her namesake, appears as a goddess with a stephane and a sceptre. On the reverse, a royal diadem is wrapped around the single cornucopia, which contains barley, a pyramidal cake, grapes and a star. Her name is also stamped on the reverse: Arsinoe Philopator, which again copies Arsinoe II's 'Arsinoe Philadelphos', referring to her status as an icon of cult as opposed to her role of queen. The coins of Arsinoe III were minted during her lifetime; however, they indicate a leap forward in terms of the promotion of the queens as goddesses. Arsinoe III's distinctive portrait type showing a mature woman with a strong profile is replicated on both her coins and portraits in the round.

On the coins her jewellery is also clearly shown in the form of earrings, a necklace and brooch.

The final amalgamation of goddess and queen is shown under Cleopatra I, who was regent to her son Ptolemy VI. The pair appeared on different sides of the same coin, in contrast to the earlier queens who appeared at the side of their consort. Cleopatra is shown with a stephane and veil, and a sceptre; this time indicated at the back of the head rather than above it. The inscription reads 'Queen Cleopatra', thus indicating that by this time the roles of queen and divinity were amalgamated, to be a queen was to be divine. Cleopatra VII, by contrast, generally appears with a broad diadem on her coins, wearing a stephane only once on coins which were minted in Cyprus to celebrate the birth of Caesarion. Here Cleopatra appears with a stephane and holds the infant child in a pose associated with the goddess Isis and her son Harpocrates, linking Cleopatra to the earlier Egyptian queens who appeared as mother of the pharaoh. All of these elements, on a coin minted in Cyprus and portraying the queen in Hellenistic Greek style, show a clever means of presentation that incorporates many references to her ancestors by the last queen of Egypt.

The various royal decrees, which were written after priestly synods, are extremely instructive with regard to the acceptance and promotion of the royal cults by the Egyptian priesthood. The Mendes stela is concerned with the deification of Arsinoe II and rituals performed by the Egyptian priests at the temple there. The decree celebrates the reception of Arsinoe as goddess and her worship in a native Egyptian capacity. Visually at the top of the stela is an offering scene in which Arsinoe and her brother make an offering to the ram-headed god of Mendes and the newly deified Arsinoe. Thus Arsinoe appears in her role as consort and goddess. Coins minted around this time show Arsinoe II with a ram's horn just below her right ear, and although they are often interpreted as the horns of the god Ammon, it is possible that they also linked her to the god of Mendes, thus emphasising her close relationship with this particular god, whom she had served as priestess in her lifetime. The Egyptian title of 'beloved of the ram' was also bestowed on Arsinoe, in addition to her other association from her lifetime with her brother as 'brother-loving'. The Pithom stela is another important source of evidence for the deification of Arsinoe II, and the placing of associated cult statues in a temple-sharing capacity. Ptolemy II decreed that a statue of his sister should be placed in every temple in Egypt. New temples were also built, such as the Arsinoeion at Memphis and in Alexandria. Ptolemy can also be found offering to his sister on the walls of the temple of Isis at Philae (Figure 17, p. 108). Arsinoe stands behind the goddess Isis, and on a gateway decorated by Ptolemy II the deified queen is also worshipped alongside Nephthys the sister of Isis. The two Egyptian goddesses are identified by the hieroglyphs of their names on the usual crowns of sun-disk and cow's horns; Arsinoe is shown with a specially designed crown which is worn by the queen when she appears as a goddess or as part of the dynastic cult. The crown is roughly based on that of the god Geb, and was later borrowed by Cleopatra VII. Such dynamic promotion of cults obviously needed financing and in order to ensure that there was enough money for the promotion of his sister's cult Ptolemy II introduced a tax on the vineyards of Egypt. Money would be fed back into the temples and so it is not difficult to see why the priests were so keen to support the ruler in the promotion of the new cult, intellectual stimulation aside. The Egyptian religion was already equipped for the promotion of a new deity, but there was also the Greek community to consider and for this a new priesthood was necessary. In Alexandria the Kanephoros of Arsinoe Philadelphos was established; *Kanephoros* literally translates as basket-carrier. Like the other priests, the priestess of the kanephoros was named in the dating formula of official documents. Temples were built in honour of the royal goddess, and in Philadelphia, in the Faiyum and also in Alexandria the shrines of Arsinoe the goddess were separate from those of Arsinoe the sibling god. A description of the temple of Arsinoe, which was housed within the palaces in Alexandria, by the ancient author Pliny in *Natural Histories*, states that there was a floating iron statue of the queen, held by magnetic force to the ceiling. Such engineering sounds unfeasible in the Ptolemaic age, but the description of the Pompe of Ptolemy II describes colossal mechanical statues supplying the revellers with wine. No remains of the temple survive and scholars typically assume that it was Greek in style. In front of the temple, however, was an obelisk that was brought to the site by Ptolemy II from Heliopolis. This act is similar to the introduction of Egyptian statuary to the essentially Greek Sarapieion in Alexandria and may have been an easy means of easing the Greeks into Egyptian culture. One hundred years later, colossal statues of the Ptolemies as Egyptians would adorn the palaces and harbour of the city. The promotion of royal cults was another relatively easy means of joining the two communities in a shared cause. Deification was not only reserved for queens; the sister of Arsinoe II, Philoteira, also received a cult and was worshipped posthumously as a goddess in her own right.

Under Ptolemy III evidence for the promotion of individual members of the royal family is explained in the texts of the trilingual Canopus decree. Like the deification of Arsinoe the decree was recorded on stelae, which were placed in the temples of Egypt in order to announce the results of the annual meeting between the king and the Egyptian priests. The Canopus and Rosetta decrees are national rather than local, and in this respect they should be distinguished from the Mendes or Pithom stela. The Canopus decree is seen to be important because it allows us an insight into the relationship between Egyptian priests and the king. For the present purposes, however, it is the second part of the decree that is most relevant, because it provides us with a detailed description of the posthumous deification of the princess Berenike, daughter of Ptolemy III and Berenike II. The decree implies that the priests inaugurated the deification of the princess Berenike and persuaded the king and queen to establish the new goddess. This essentially translates into a financial agreement, whereby the rulers would pay for the deification of their daughter as well as agreeing to the actual deification. The princess was laid out at Canopus, and rituals that are compared in the decree to those of the mourning ceremonies of the Apis and Mnervis bulls were enacted. An annual festival which, it states, was to be celebrated with a procession of boats in the usual Egyptian fashion was then established in honour of the princess. We are also told that a divine statue of gold and inlaid with stones was to be placed in every temple in Egypt. A priest within each temple was then allocated to the care of the statue. It is also stated that the gold crown that was to be placed on the head of the statue of Berenike was different to that placed on the head of her mother, the female pharaoh Berenike. The crown consisted of two ears of wheat with a stalk of papyrus behind and a uraeus in front; it is then specifically noted that the tail of the uraeus should be entwined around the papyrus so that the crown reads 'Berenike'. A festival linked to that of Osiris (which was the time when Berenike died) is then mentioned, and that a second statue should be made and should receive the first harvest of each year from the priestesses. The careful attention to detail by the Egyptian priests illustrates a care that goes beyond that of duty as they throw themselves into the necessary rituals and plans for the deification of the princess Berenike. Neither the princess Berenike, nor indeed any other Ptolemaic queen was awarded the honour of appearing with the divinities on the walls of temples. Arsinoe is in this respect quite unique. The Greek-style representation of the deceased child with her mother, as mentioned in Chapter 4 (Figure 10, p. 82), suggests that the death was at least marked among the Greek communities, if not remembered in such a spectacular fashion.

The most famous of all, the Rosetta decree, is better known for its place in the history of the decipherment of the hieroglyphic script than as an important historical document. It is, however, of considerable consequence for our knowledge of Ptolemaic royal cults and the placing of statues within the temples of other gods. The introduction of Sunnaoi Theoi, or temple-sharing gods, was associated with the dynastic cult, and occurs in both Greek and Egyptian contexts. The decrees demonstrate, to some degree, that representations of rulers in a temple-sharing capacity were regulated by the state or temples. However, private initiative seems also to have been a factor in the dedication of an image within a specific temple, as indicated by petitions requesting permission to dedicate statues on behalf of the royal house. In most cases the individual is honouring the ruler and making the offering to a god, not to the deified ruler. However, there are instances where even members of the royal family invoke the divine ruler, as recorded in the *Lock of Berenike*, where Berenike II invokes Arsinoe Aphrodite.

Berenike II's own deification was posthumous and her promotion by her son meant that although she was not awarded the same honours as Arsinoe on Egyptian temple reliefs, she was nevertheless promoted over her predecessor. This is seen clearly in the dating formulae, where her priestesses are placed before those of the Kanephoroi, when in actual fact the chronological sequence ought to have been respected. Berenike II appears on some of the faience oinochoai that were manufactured during the reign of Ptolemy IV. She can be distinguished from the current queen Arsinoe III by her stephane and also to a limited degree by the different portrait features. On one example, often identified as Cleopatra I but more recently as Berenike II on stylistic grounds, the subject wears a knotted garment and a corkscrew wig. These particular features became markers of a divine queen.

Cleopatra I appeared as a divine queen on coinage minted to celebrate her regency with her son. The titles of dating formulae also call the queen *Thea* or goddess, and by this time the two roles were closely associated. It is also during this period that we see a decrease in Greek-style representations and an increase in those made according to Egyptian canons but with features that would enable a Greek to read the representation. The statues first appear in the third century BC, no doubt to coincide with the deification of Arsinoe II in 270/69 BC. They come from the Egyptian tradition in which the costume has a knot securing the dress either between the breasts or above the

Figure 21 *Fragment of an Egyptian-style statue of an early Cleopatra, from Alexandria. (Greco-Roman Museum, Alexandria 21992. Photograph by Sally-Ann Ashton.)*

left breast. As many of the earliest examples have lost their heads, it is not possible to know how their hair was styled, but certainly from the time of Berenike II the images are often shown with the Libyan corkscrew wig rather than the traditional Egyptian tripartite wig. The examples that are stylistically early do not hold a cornucopia, but are shown with either ankh signs or enigmatic bars clenched in their hands; the arms are held firmly by their sides. The statues offer further evidence for the understanding of the various royal cults and religious patronage. The development of statue types representing the queens in their deified form is extremely clever in that they are effectively bilingual, representing the bicultural interest in the deification and promotion of the royal cults and also helping to distinguish between queen or consort and goddess.

Figure 22 *Fragment of an Egyptian-style statue of Arsinoe III. (Ny Carlsberg Glyptotek, Copenhagen IN 581. Photograph copyright and reproduced with permission of the Ny Carlsberg Glyptotek.)*

A large limestone head from such a statue was found in the Mazarita region of Alexandria and probably represents an early Cleopatra (Figure 21). The hair is parted down the middle and there are thick locks that fall onto the shoulders. This particular hairstyle required a bun at the back of the head but, of course, on this Egyptian statue the back pillar to the top of the head prevented this. Not to be deterred, the artist has indicated a sort of upward curl on either side of the pillar thus giving an artistic representation of the style if not the real thing. That such an image with uraeus and a crown of cobras, which would have supported an Egyptian headdress, should have been found in Alexandria indicates a continued presence of Egyptian culture in the capital city. This head possibly belongs to a subgroup that is of considerable interest. There is small group of images that may have been intended as parallels for the images of male rulers as Greek

135

Figure 23 *Fragment of an Egyptian-style statue of an early Cleopatra. (Ny Carlsberg Glyptotek, Copenhagen 1472. Photograph copyright and reproduced with permission of the Ny Carlsberg Glyptotek.)*

pharaohs. Most of the Egyptian-style representations of Ptolemaic royal women are of a stylised nature, but in the Ny Carlsberg Glyptotek in Copenhagen there is one head, a fragment from a statue that is made from a hard Egyptian stone (basalt) and has a Greek-style hairstyle and portrait features (Figure 22, p. 135). The portrait is identified as Arsinoe III on account of the hairstyle, which is rolled up at the sides and pulled into a bun. The fashion of showing the rulers in the guise of an Egyptian pharaoh, but with portrait features that are more typical of the Greek tradition, began during the reign of Ptolemy V. This portrait of Arsinoe may be an early example, perhaps manufactured before her death. Its existence may indicate quite a change in the ideology of queenship, and it is of particular interest that similar images were also made of Cleopatras II and III. Another basalt head in Copenhagen shows a queen with por-

Figure 24 *Inscribed Egyptian-style statue of Arsinoe II.*
(The Metropolitan Museum of Art, New York Rogers Fund, 1920
(20.2.22). All rights reserved, The Metropolitan Museum of Art.)

trait features that are similar to those of Ptolemy VIII. The modius (support) on top of the head would probably have been originally designed as a circlet of royal cobras. Such images were probably used in cities such as Alexandria, and indeed the existence of the Mazarita limestone head supports this idea.

This basalt head (Figure 23, p. 136) which may represent Cleopatra II on account of its similarity to the portraits of Ptolemy VIII, also shows an essentially Egyptian-style statue adopting a Greek coiffure. Here, the hair was unfinished but the uraeus and styling of the piece place it within an Egyptian workshop. The appearance of these bi-lingual images during the early second century BC is indicative of a wider move towards acculturation and in many respects was the culmination of the policies of Ptolemy II to present Egyptian-style images to the Greeks. A similar statue in terms of the facial features is perhaps the most important from this group of images because it is inscribed (Figure 24). The Metropolitan Museum of Art's statue of Arsinoe shows the queen with the full regalia: a knotted costume, a cornucopia and a corkscrew wig. The back pillar, which is rather worn, states that the image is of Arsinoe and most importantly she is associated with the god Amun. I stress this point because of the erroneous association of this iconography in the Ptolemaic period with the goddess Isis, although the more direct association of Cleopatra III with the goddess goes a long way towards explaining how this link was later made.

Cleopatra III and Cleopatra VII are both extremely important individuals in the historical development of the divine queen. Both believed themselves to be the goddess Isis, and Cleopatra III, above all other queens, was keen to promote herself as a divine being. Hölbl suggests that the elevation of Cleopatra III as 'Isis, the great one, mother of the gods' was intended to surpass the status of her mother, with whom she ruled as part of the unhappy triad of king, mother and wife. Cleopatra III also set up three further priesthoods to serve her as a goddess, and so from 116 BC there was the garland-bearer of

Figure 25 *Fragment of an Egyptian-style statue of Cleopatra III. (Kunsthistorisches Museum, Vienna I 406. Copyright and reproduced with permission of the Kunsthistorisches Museum, Vienna.)*

139

Figure 26 *Colossal Egyptian-style statue of Cleopatra II or III , from Alexandria. (Greco-Roman Museum, Alexandria. Photograph by Sally-Ann Ashton.)*

Figure 27 *Sphinx with the head of Cleopatra III, Narmouthis. (Source: Author.)*

Cleopatra, the light-bearer and the priestess. Cleopatra also placed herself before the cults of Arsinoe and Berenike in the dating formula.

The images of the deified Cleopatra III are some of the most powerful in the Ptolemaic repertoire. On one particular head

140

from an Egyptian-style statue the queen adopts the portrait features of her sons, and it is probably safe to say that this portrait dates to the period of her co-rule with either Ptolemy IX or Ptolemy X (Figure 25). We essentially see a man's portrait in the guise of the queen, which aptly represents Cleopatra's desires. These images are the closest Ptolemaic equivalent to Hatshepsut. Around this time we also see a strong political statement outside the Pharos (lighthouse) of Alexandria in the form of what is believed to be up to four representations of royal pairs, indicating that statues with knotted garments had replaced the more traditional Egyptian-style images for the dynastic cult. The best-preserved statue shows either Cleopatra II or Cleopatra III wearing the knotted costume, corkscrew wig and holding a cornucopia (Figure 26). The accompanying male rulers had Greek-style portraits, thus showing themselves as Greek pharaohs and their queens as divine. This line-up would have been one of the first sights as boats sailed into the Alexandrian harbour; as a group they served an important political as well as religious function. Further along the coast, at Herakleion, another group of colossal representations has been found, together with a stela with texts in hieroglyphic and Greek script. The group shows the god Hapi, a queen possibly forming a protective divine pair on either side of a late Ptolemaic ruler.

Another statue of this particular queen is of further interest because it clearly illustrates her elevated status on two different levels (Figure 27). The statue is in the form of a sphinx, which marks the dromos, or processional walkway, of a temple at Narmouthis in the Faiyum. The sphinxes have the heads of male rulers, as was often the case in earlier periods of Egyptian history, but one shows the portrait of Cleopatra III. More unusual is the dress that is worn by the queen: between the breasts is a knotted garment, perhaps hinting at her divine as well as royal status. Sphinxes with female portrait heads are extremely rare and for this particular queen to appear in such a prominent position alongside her co-rulers allows us to see her true status, even outside Alexandria.

As previously noted, there was no doubt about the status of Cleopatra VII; from early in her reign she took the title *Thea* or goddess, but this divine role is often part of her queenship. It seems that the ultimate self-deification was to become Isis and this was certainly how the queen was shown in the Hadra sanctuary discussed in the earlier part of this chapter. There are statues with a triple uraeus from the divine as well as the royal categories, showing that the queen (here thought to be Cleopatra VII but considered by others to represent Cleopatra III) was still represented in both forms. Whether the increase of the 'divine' images was also intended to show the elevated status of many of these queens is not known. Their development and continued use as a specific group, however, is another example of an initiative by the Egyptian priesthood to adapt to a slightly different form of ruler.

The dynastic and the individual cults of queens were prevalent in terms of associated representations in both Greek and Egyptian contexts. As with the dynastic cult, individual cults were controlled by the state and were promoted throughout Egypt rather than being confined to Alexandria. In many instances the evidence for royal representations echoes the developments in the dynastic cult, and the statues of queens, when considered alongside the decrees, also shed light on the intended nuances of these complicated associations between the various rulers and established deities. The religious policies of the Ptolemaic royal house are important in the understanding of the images of rulers that were produced and promoted by the court. The continued use of many of these representations after the fall of the dynasty can almost certainly be linked to the association between the later Ptolemaic queens and Isis.

CHAPTER 7

The legacy of the Ptolemaic queens

Promotion of the Ptolemaic royal cause did not end with the death of Cleopatra VII in 30 BC. Cleopatra's eldest son, Caesarion, disappears from the historical record and was no doubt eliminated by Octavian – if not personally, then by his supporters. Mark Antony's children were, however, spared. Octavia, Mark Antony's widow and sister of Octavian, brought up the three remaining children but, like Caesarion, the boys Alexander Helios and Ptolemy Philadelphos are not mentioned as adults, although it is thought that Cleopatra Selene took them with her to Mauritania. The princess was married to a client king of Rome, Juba II of Mauritania (modern Algeria), and moved to the capital Cherchel. Cleopatra Selene and Juba II had one child, a boy named Ptolemy who suffered a fate that was familiar to his Egyptian ancestors: he was murdered. In true Ptolemaic fashion he died on account of his party dress which, it was claimed, enraged the emperor Caligula because it was better than the Roman's own attire. In reality the emperor's half-cousin (for he too was descended from Mark Antony) posed a political threat.

It is interesting that among the material from the palaces in Cherchel there are Egyptian statues that were brought from Egypt, perhaps to remind Cleopatra Selene of her identity.

Occasional fragments of Egyptianising relief have also been found at the site, but the overall appearance followed the Roman ethos with copies of Greek sculpture adorning the gardens and living areas. There is, of course, the portrait head of Cleopatra from Cherchel, although scholars are divided as to whether this particular image represents mother or daughter.

Juba minted coins with an Egyptian crown on the reverse, or the same crown accompanied by an Egyptian *sistrum* (rattle). This was not just any Egyptian crown, however, but that worn by Ptolemaic queens. In catalogues of such coins the double plume, cow's horns and sun-disk is referred to as the crown of Isis. Technically speaking, however, Isis continued to wear the usual cow's horns and sun-disk headdress as seen on temple reliefs from Philae. Such confusion, or perhaps deliberate promotion, led to a more fundamental mistake on behalf of the Romans: the re-use of statues representing deified Ptolemaic queens to represent Isis.

The development of the iconography of Isis is a slow but fascinating phenomenon and in terms of promotion it is difficult to see how the Ptolemaic queens could have formed a more successful campaign had they meticulously planned it. Initially, the Romans struggle with an iconography for the goddess, who is associated with several gods in order to represent her different roles within Egyptian theology. In the Egyptian tradition gods are adaptable and often change their roles. Greek and Roman ideologies meant that gods could be joined to define a key role more clearly, but it was not possible for Athena, for example, to suddenly take on the role associated with Aphrodite. When posed with the problem of different meanings and associations of Isis, the Romans simply added a qualifying goddess or title; Isis Palagia, for example, was associated with the sea. Like many of the Ptolemaic statues from Egypt, the Roman representations of Isis are often without a firm provenance or date and so it is difficult to know when iconography changed or developed, and under which ruler. However, there are some obvious candidates from within the Roman Imperial families.

144

When considering the history of Isis in Italy it must be remembered that the Triumviri had dedicated a temple to the goddess and her consort Sarapis in honour of Julius Caesar; this was housed either on the Capitoline Hill or the Campus Martius. There is also the two-year presence of Cleopatra VII in Rome to be added to the equation, and the marble head of an Egyptian goddess that was found in an area known to house an early sanctuary of Egyptian gods may well represent the last queen (see front cover).

Octavian, who later became Augustus, used Egyptian imagery to promote his victory over Cleopatra and Mark Antony, most notably by including two obelisks outside his Mausoleum in Rome. Takács, in a study of Isis and Sarapis in the Roman world, notes that from the Late Republican repertoire the Nilotic landscape continued to be integrated into the Imperial artistic tradition, duplicated unintentionally and unconsciously. The Roman love for things exotic, however, was probably quite intentional, in a similar way to the many buildings called Africa House or India House in British cities, with imagery that epitomised British colonies and dominions for the British viewers, who had never left their country. The hippopotamus-infested Nile, complete with pygmies and marsh-dwellers, that adorned mosaics and wall paintings was probably no closer to Roman Egypt than it is to Egypt today. Initiates to the Isiac cults in Rome during the Late Republican period would also have been keen advocates for Egyptian or rather Egyptianising objects. The worship of Isis suffered a setback during the reign of Tiberius, however, when there was a scandal at the Iseum in Rome. Priests were crucified and the statues from the sanctuary were thrown into the river Tiber (Josephus, *Antiquitates Judaicae* 18.66–80).

A modern biographer writing on the life of Gaius Caesar (Caligula) suggested that his grandmother influenced his interest in Egypt and the Orient and as such he was a prime candidate for the promotion of Egyptian cults. The extent of his interest in Egyptian cults is not certain. There remains a question mark over the identity of the instigator of the Iseum Campense, one of Rome's largest Isea. There is little evidence of his interest in

Egypt, but this has not prevented some scholars from suggesting that Caligula was responsible for the early building of the site; others regard early activity at the sight as a private rather than public venture.

Similarly, the emperors Claudius and Nero do not seem to have taken an active interest in Egyptian cults, although there are several portraits that have been identified as one or the other, manufactured in the Egyptian style but showing their usual portrait features. Under Vespasian, however, there was a renewed promotion of the god Sarapis (who became the consort of Isis in both Greek and Roman traditions). Vespasian had been in Egypt when he was declared emperor and was said to have performed miracles at the sanctuary of Sarapis in Alexandria. Or, a more cynical interpretation would be that Vespasian selected this god and then performed miracles to cement the relationship. During the Flavian dynasty Isis and Sarapis became state gods and were promoted as such. As part of this renewed interest, Vespasian expanded the Iseum Campense. However, he seems to have been keener to associate himself with Sarapis because of the miracles at this particular god's sanctuary.

In 79 AD Mount Vesuvius erupted and Pompeii was destroyed, or rather preserved beneath the ash from the volcano. A temple to Isis at Pompeii was rebuilt fifteen years before the eruption, in 64 AD, and provides important evidence for the development of the cult of Isis at this point in Roman history. Images from the sanctuary are not Egyptian, but follow either classical or archaic Greek styles. Greek-style representations of Isis are common in the early part of the first century AD, and other examples have been found in Greece, most notably on the island of Delos.

The people of Italy were obviously familiar with the Ptolemaic queens, and from a private villa at Herculaneum called the Villa of Papyri, a bronze portrait of a Ptolemaic queen was found alongside other royal portraits that must have formed part of a decorative group within the house. The image is striking and is a tantalising impression of the many bronze statues that were lost in antiquity, usually melted down and re-used. The queen wears her hair in tight corkscrew locks and is similar in many respects to marble images of the second-century BC Cleopatras. The Herculaneum queen wears a thin diadem that was perhaps a copy of an original Ptolemaic image brought to Rome for part of Octavian's victory parade. It is a quite remarkable image.

It was really only during the reign of Domitian (81–96 AD) that Isis rose to greater prominence in Italy. The change in iconography and the adoption of imagery which, in actual fact, represented a deified Ptolemaic queen seems to have occurred on a national level and was without doubt promoted by the Imperial house. Two main sanctuaries can be associated with Domitian: the aforementioned Iseum Campense in Rome and another temple of Isis at Benevento in southern Italy. At Benevento there are several statues – made from marble and in a Roman style – which show a female wearing the knotted garment once worn by the Ptolemaic queens. Of course, dedications at both sanctuaries may well have been made after Domitian's reign but there is further, more securely datable evidence from both Italy and Egypt to suggest that it was under this particular emperor that the iconography of Isis in the Roman world was developed.

Lamps that are traditionally dated from 40 to 90 AD are decorated with the bust of a female figure wearing a crown of cow's horns, sun-disk and plumes and with a prominent knot between the breasts (Figure 28). The hairstyles are slightly unkempt with strands falling onto the shoulders. Ptolemaic royal iconography was not only used by association to represent Isis, but statues of queens were brought to Italy from Egypt and displayed in sanctuaries as representations of Isis. What greater prize for the personal shrine or sanctuary of a devotee of the cult than an image of a Ptolemaic queen, who, it must be remembered, was believed to be Isis?

When a survey of surviving Isis statues is undertaken, interesting discrepancies in attributes can be found, possibly reflecting the different roles of the goddess and her associations with

Figure 28 *Handle from a Roman oil-lamp showing a bust of Isis. (The Petrie Museum of Egyptian Archaeology University College London. Image copyright and reproduced with permission of the Petrie Museum of Egyptian Archaeology.)*

148

existing Roman deities, but also perhaps as a result of the different types of image used for the Ptolemaic queens. Some have a cornucopia; others hold a sistrum and situla (rattle and ceremonial vessel). In terms of their hairstyle some are shown with corkscrew locks while others wear their hair loosely tied in a bun with strands of hair falling onto their shoulders. The majority are executed in marble, but small terracotta or bronze figures were also commonly made and probably taken from or given to sanctuaries of the goddess. The problem with many of these representations is that their provenance has been lost, which also means that they are difficult to date and we do not know whether the changes in style and iconography were chronological or geographical.

The traditional Egyptian-style representations of Ptolemaic queens were also imported to Italy and copied, as illustrated by the Vatican Arsinoe (Figure 16, p. 104), which was found in the Gardens of Sallust in Rome along with two other Ptolemaic statues. One was the second from the pair with Arsinoe II, representing her brother and consort, Ptolemy II Philadelphos. The other was a second female figure that was substantially repaired during the Roman period. Interestingly the same sculptor repaired the arm of the Arsinoe statue to form the same unusual pose in which the queen holds a piece of cloth. The date of the transportation of this group is unknown, but scholars generally suggest that they appeared in Rome during the reign of either Caligula or Hadrian, and the latter seems a more likely candidate.

There are several instances of copies of Ptolemaic original statues under the emperor Hadrian, most notably from his villa at Tivoli, which is just outside Rome. Hadrian did more than simply use Egyptian sculpture, he embraced it with open arms and with a new set of ideals that have resulted in many Hadrianic pieces being denounced by today's Egyptologists as forgeries from the eighteenth or nineteenth century. Images of Ptolemaic queens were used as models for a new form of statue that can only really be described as Egyptianising in terms of its style.

Images of Isis still wear the knotted garment but were made in dark marble to imitate the hard Egyptian stone rather than the marble versions that were produced under Domitian. The Hadrianic statues also revert to a more traditional model for their form in that copies of the traditional tripartite wig appear in the Roman repertoire for the first time. Such developments stem from what seems to have been a genuine attempt to under-stand aspects of Egyptian religion and art. At Tivoli a group of black marble statues replicate a little known cult of Isis-Apis from Memphis and are profoundly different to the earlier attempts by Domitian to present 'Egyptian' cults to Italy. What is perhaps the most revealing aspect of the Tivoli statues is that they are from the private rather than public domain.

The cult of Isis also experienced a renaissance during Hadrian's rule, partly because of her adoption by the empress Sabine, who was the first Imperial wife to become actively associated with the goddess. The Imperial couple travelled to Egypt in 130–131 AD, and stayed there for 10 months. This visit had a profound effect on Hadrian and, together, the pair were presented and promoted in both Egypt and Italy as Sarapis and Isis. The sanctuary of Sarapis in Alexandria was rebuilt, with a greater emphasis on the god's Egyptian origins in terms of architectural elements in Egyptian granite and a small sanctuary dedicated to the Apis bull (Sarapis being a Greek version of the Egyptian god Osiris-Apis).

The final step in the process of the Romanisation of Isis, however, can be found at a small temple that was built at Luxor, dating to 124 AD. The building was essentially Roman in character, but with an Egyptian cornice at the top. Three gods were honoured in the sanctuary: Zeus Helios, Sarapis and Isis, who was the only traditional Egyptian deity of the three to be included. When we consider the cult statue of the goddess from the site (Figure 29) we find a white marble Roman ver-sion of the goddess, wearing a knotted garment of a classical style, based on the images that Ptolemaic queens had adopted 400 years earlier.

Figure 29 *Cult statue from the Temple of Zeus Helios, Sarapis and Isis, Luxor. (Photograph and copyright Sally-Ann Ashton.)*

The queens themselves continued to be worshipped as goddesses in Egypt following the Roman conquest. The last reference that we have to a statue of a Ptolemaic queen dates to 373 AD. A text written in the cursive Egyptian script of Demotic by a scribe named Petesenufe states 'I overlaid the figure of Cleopatra with gold'.

A selective family tree of the Ptolemaic queens

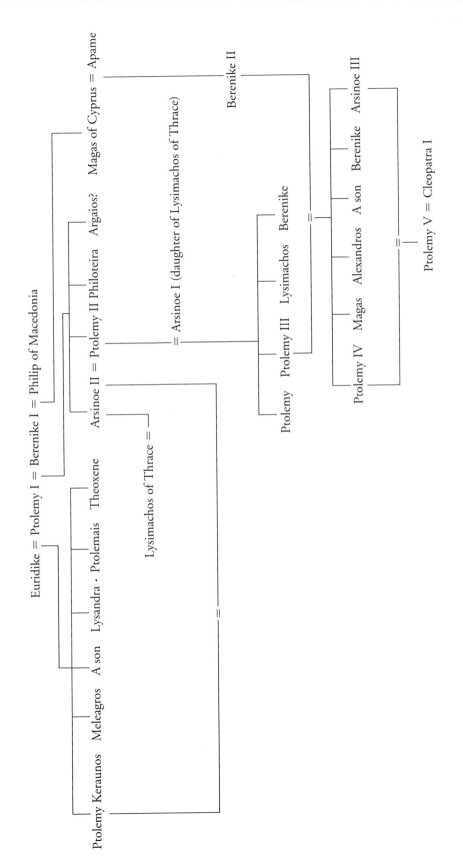

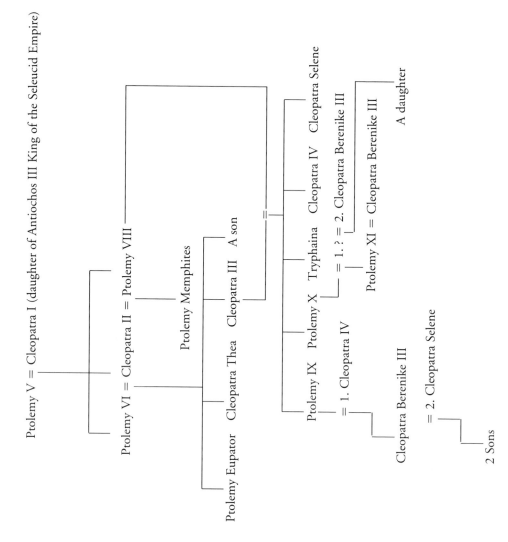

Ptolemy V = Cleopatra I (daughter of Antiochos III King of the Seleucid Empire)

Ptolemy VI = Cleopatra II = Ptolemy VIII

Ptolemy Eupator   Cleopatra Thea   Cleopatra III   A son

Ptolemy Memphites

Ptolemy IX   Ptolemy X   Tryphaina   Cleopatra IV   Cleopatra Selene
= 1. Cleopatra IV

= 1. ? = 2. Cleopatra Berenike III

Ptolemy XI = Cleopatra Berenike III

Cleopatra Berenike III

A daughter

= 2. Cleopatra Selene

2 Sons

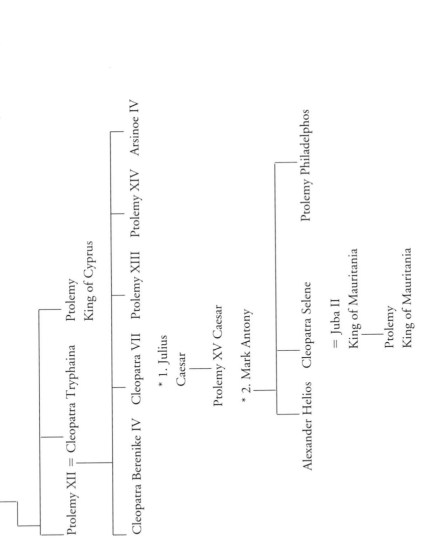

*3.?

Ptolemy XII = Cleopatra Tryphaina   Ptolemy
                                     King of Cyprus

Cleopatra Berenike IV   Cleopatra VII   Ptolemy XIII   Ptolemy XIV   Arsinoe IV

                         * 1. Julius
                              Caesar

                         Ptolemy XV Caesar

                         * 2. Mark Antony

Alexander Helios   Cleopatra Selene   Ptolemy Philadelphos

                    = Juba II
                      King of Mauritania

                         Ptolemy
                         King of Mauritania

Note: **Cleopatra VII, Ptolemy XIII, Ptolemy XIV and Arsinoe IV may be the children of an unknown mother (see Hölbl);**
* = not officially married

Bibliography and sources

Chapter 1

C. Aldred, *Akhenaten and Nefertiti.* New York: The Brooklyn Museum, 1973.

J. Allen, 'Akhenaten's "Mystery" co-regent and successor', *Amarna Letters. Essays on Ancient Egypt, c. 1390–1310 BC*, 1: 74–85. San Francisco: Sebastopol CAKMY Communications, 1991.

D. Arnold (ed.), *The Royal Women of Amarna. Images of Beauty from Ancient Egypt.* New York: The Metropolitan Museum of Art, 1997.

S.-A. Ashton, 'The double and triple uraeus and Egyptian royal women', in A. Cooke and F. Simpson (eds) *Current Research in Egyptology 2001.* Oxford: Archaeopress, forthcoming.

B.M. Bryan, 'In women good and bad fortune are on earth. Status and roles of women in Egyptian culture', in G.E. Markoe and K. Capel (eds) *Mistress of the House, Mistress of Heaven : Women in Ancient Egypt.* New York: Hudson Hills, Press, 1996.

H. Gauthier, *Le livre des rois d'Égypte: Recueil de titres et protocoles royaux, noms propres de rois, reines, princes, princesses et parents de rois, 4: De la XXVe Dynastie à la fin des Ptolémées.* Cairo: MIFAO 20, 1916.

W. Grajetzki, *Digital Egypt Website*. http://www.petrie.ucl.ac.uk/ digital_egypt/Welcome.html

L. Green ,'The royal women of Amarna: who was who?', in D. Arnold (ed.) *The Royal Women of Amarna. Images of Beauty from Ancient Egypt.* New York: The Metropolitan Museum of Art, 1997.

G.E. Markoe and K. Capel (eds), *Mistress of the House, Mistress of Heaven : Women in Ancient Egypt.* New York: Hudson Hills Press, 1996.

B. Porter and R.L.B. Moss, *A Topographical Bibliography of Ancient Egyptian Hieroglyphic Texts, Reliefs and Paintings.* Several volumes. Oxford: Oxford University Press.

G. Robins, *Women in Ancient Egypt.* London: British Museum Press, 1993.

I. Shaw (ed.) *Oxford History of Ancient Egypt.* Oxford: Oxford University Press, 2000.

L. Troy, *Patterns of Queenship in Ancient Egyptian Myth and History.* Uppsala Studies in Ancient Mediterranean and Near Eastern Civilisations 14. Uppsala: Boreas, 1986.

Chapter 2

D. Arnold, *Temples of the Last Pharaohs.* New York: Oxford University Press, 1999.

S.-A. Ashton, *Ptolemaic Royal Sculpture from Egypt: The Interaction between Greek and Egyptian Traditions.* Oxford: Archaeopress, 2001.

S.-A. Ashton, *Petrie's Ptolemaic and Roman Memphis* (forthcoming).

S.-A. Ashton, 'Foreigners at Memphis? Petrie's racial types', in W.J. Tait (ed.) *Never Had the Like Occurred: Egypt's View of its Past.* University of Pennsylvania Press (forthcoming).

S.-A. Ashton, 'The Ptolemaic royal image and the Egyptian tradition', in W.J. Tait (ed.) *Never Had the Like Occurred: Egypt's View of its Past.* University of Pennsylvania Press (forthcoming).

A.K. Bowman, *Egypt After the Pharaohs.* Oxford: Oxford University Press, 1996 (repr.).

J.-Y. Empereur, *Alexandria Rediscovered*. London: British Museum Press, 1998.

H.W. Fairman (ed.), *The Triumph of Horus*. London: Batsford, 1974.

P.M. Fraser, *Ptolemaic Alexandria*. Oxford: Oxford University Press, 1972, reprinted 1998.

F. Goddio et al., *Alexandria. The Submerged Royal Quarters*. London: Periplus, 1998.

P. Green (ed.), *Alexandria and Alexandrianism*. Papers delivered at a symposium organized by the J. Paul Getty Museum and the Getty Center for the History of Art and the Humanities and held at the Museum, April 22–25, 1993. Malibu: J.P. Getty Museum, 1996.

J.H. Johnson (ed.), *Life in a Multi-cultural Society: Egypt from Cambyses to Constantine and Beyond*. Chicago: Oriental Institute of Chicago, 1992.

J.-Ph. Lauer and C. Picard, *Les statues ptolémaïques du Sarapieion de Memphis*. Paris: Presses Universitaires de France, 1955.

N. Lewis, *Greeks in Ptolemaic Egypt: Case Studies in the Social History of the Hellenistic World*. Oxford: Clarendon, 1986.

S.B. Pomeroy, *Women in Hellenistic Egypt. From Alexander to Cleopatra*. Detroit: Wayne State University Press, 1990 (repr.).

E. Rice, *The Grand Procession of Ptolemy Philadelphus*. Oxford: Oxford University Press, 1983.

A. Rowe, *Discovery of the Famous Temple Enclosure of Serapis at Alexandria*. London, 1946.

J. Rowlandson (ed.), *Women and Society in Greek and Roman Egypt: a Sourcebook*. Cambridge: Cambridge University Press, 1998.

R.R.R. Smith, *Hellenistic Royal Portraits*. Oxford: Oxford University Press, 1988.

B. Tkaczow, *Topography of Ancient Alexandria (An Archaeological Map)*. Warsaw: Travaux Du Centre D'Archéologie Méditerranéenne de l'Académie Polonaise Des Sciences, vol. 32, 1993.

D.J. Thompson, *Memphis Under the Ptolemies.* Princeton: Princeton University Press, 1988.

D.J. Thompson, 'Philadelphus' Procession Dynastic Power in a Mediterranean Context', in L. Mooren (ed.) *Politics, Administration and Society in the Hellenistic and Roman World: Proceedings of the International Colloquium, Bertinoro 19–24 July 1997.* Studia Hellenistica, 36. Leuven: Peeters, 2000: 365–88.

L.V. Zabkar, *Hymns to Isis in her Temple at Philae.* Hanover, New Hampshire: University Press of New England, 1988.

Chapter 3

M.M. Austin, *The Hellenistic World from Alexander to the Roman Conquest. A Selection of Ancient Sources in Translation.* Cambridge: Cambridge University Press, 1981.

G. Hölbl, *A History of the Ptolemaic Empire.* New York: Routledge, 2001.

P.M. Fraser, *Ptolemaic Alexandria.* Oxford: Oxford University Press, 1972; reprinted 1998.

M. Grant, *Cleopatra.* New York: Barnes & Noble, 1972; reprinted 1995.

P. Green, *From Alexander to Actium. The Hellenistic Age.* London: Thames & Hudson, 1990.

J.G. Griffiths, 'The Death of Cleopatra VII', *JEA* 47, 1961: 113–18.

E.S. Gruen, *The Hellenistic World and the Coming of Rome.* California: University of California Press, 1984.

M. Hamer, *Signs of Cleopatra: History, Politics, Representation.* London; New York: Routledge, 1992.

S.B. Pomeroy, *Women in Hellenistic Egypt. From Alexander to Cleopatra.* Detroit: Wayne State University Press, 1990 (repr.).

C.B.R. Pelling, *Life of Antony.* Cambridge: Cambridge University Press, 1988.

F.W. Walbank, *The Hellenistic World.* London: Fontana, 1981.

S. Walker, 'Cleopatra's images: reflections of reality', in S. Walker and P. Higgs, *Cleopatra of Egypt: From History to Myth.* London: British Museum Press, 2001: 142–47.

S. Walker and P. Higgs, *Cleopatra of Egypt: From History to Myth*. London: British Museum Press, 2001.

J. Whitehorne, *Cleopatras*. London: Routledge, 1994.

G. Weil-Goudchaux, 'Was Cleopatra beautiful? The conflicting answers of numismatics', in S. Walker and P. Higgs, *Cleopatra of Egypt: From History to Myth*. London: British Museum Press, 2001: 210–15.

J.H.C. Williams, 'Spoiling the Egyptians: Octavian and Cleopatra', in S. Walker and P. Higgs, *Cleopatra of Egypt: From History to Myth*. London: British Museum Press, 2001: 190–9.

Chapter 4

R.S. Bianchi (ed.), *Cleopatra's Egypt: Age of the Ptolemies*. Brooklyn: Brooklyn Museum, 1988.

N. Davis and C.M. Kraay, *The Hellenistic Kingdoms: Portrait Coins and History*. London: Thames & Hudson, 1990.

P.M. Fraser, *Ptolemaic Alexandria*. Oxford: Oxford University Press, 1972; reprinted 1998.

P. Higgs, 'Searching for Cleopatra's image: classical portraits in stone', in S. Walker and P. Higgs, *Cleopatra of Egypt: From History to Myth*. London: British Museum Press. 2001: 200–09.

H. Kyrieleis, *Bildnisse der Ptolemäer*. Berlin: AF 2, 1974.

K. Lemke, 'Eine Ptolemäergalerie aus Thmuis/Tell Timai', *Jahrbuch des Deutschen Archäologischen Instituts,* Band 115 (2000): 113–46.

G.H. Macurdy, *Hellenistic Queens: A Study of Woman-Power in Macedonia, Seleucid Syria and Ptolemaic Egypt*. Baltimore: The Johns Hopkins Press, 1932.

A. Meadows, 'Sins of the fathers: the inheritance of Cleopatra, the last queen of Egypt', in S. Walker and P. Higgs, *Cleopatra of Egypt: From History to Myth*. London: British Museum Press, 2001: 14–31.

J.G. Milne, 'Ptolemaic seal impressions', *Journal of Hellenic Studies* 36, 1916: 87–101.

S.B. Pomeroy, *Women in Hellenistic Egypt. From Alexander to Cleopatra.* Detroit: Wayne State University Press, 1990 (repr.).

R.R.R. Smith, *Hellenistic Royal Portraits.* Oxford: Oxford University Press, 1988; reprinted 1998.

D.B. Thompson, *Ptolemaic Oinochoai and Portraits in Faience, Aspects of the Ruler-Cult.* Oxford: Oxford University Press, 1973.

A.J.B Wace et al., *Hermopolis Magna, Ashmunein – The Ptolemaic Sanctuary and Basilica.* Alexandria, 1959.

S. Walker and P. Higgs, *Cleopatra of Egypt: From History to Myth.* London: British Museum Press, 2001.

Chapter 5

D. Arnold, *Temples of the Last Pharaohs.* New York: Oxford University Press, 1999.

S.-A. Ashton, 'Identifying the Egyptian-style Ptolemaic queens', in S. Walker and P. Higgs, *Cleopatra of Egypt: From History to Myth.* London: British Museum Press, 2001: 148–52.

S.-A. Ashton, *Ptolemaic Royal Sculpture from Egypt: The Interaction between Greek and Egyptian Traditions.* Oxford: Archaeopress, 2001.

R.S. Bianchi (ed.), *Cleopatra's Egypt: Age of the Ptolemies.* Brooklyn: Brooklyn Museum, 1988.

B.V. Bothmer, *Egyptian Sculpture of the Late Period.* Brooklyn: Brooklyn Museum, 1960.

P. Dils, 'La couronne d'Arsinoé II Philadelphe', in W. Clarysse et al. (eds.) *Egyptian Religion, The Last Thousand Years: Studies Dedicated to the Memory of Jan Quaegebeur,* vol. 2. Leuven: OLA 85, 1998: 1309–30.

G. Hölbl, *A History of the Ptolemaic Empire.* New York: Routledge, 2001.

B. Porter and R.L.B. Moss, *A Topographical Bibliography of Ancient Egyptian Hieroglyphic Texts, Reliefs, and Paintings.* Several volumes. Oxford: Oxford University Press.

D. Svenson, 'Darstellungen Hellenistischer Könige mit Götterattributen'. *Archäologische Studien,* Band 10. Frankfurt, 1995.

L. Troy, *Patterns of Queenship in Ancient Egyptian Myth and History*. Uppsala Studies in Ancient Mediterranean and Near Eastern Civilisations 14. Uppsala: Boreas, 1986.

S. Walker and P. Higgs, *Cleopatra of Egypt: From History to Myth*. London: British Museum Press, 2001.

Chapter 6

S.-A. Ashton, *Ptolemaic Royal Sculpture from Egypt: The Interaction between Greek and Egyptian Traditions*. Oxford: Archaeopress, 2001.

S.-A. Ashton, 'The Ptolemaic influence on Egyptian royal statuary', in A. McDonald and C. Riggs (eds.) *Current Research in Egyptology*. Oxford: Archaeopress, 2000: 1–11.

R.S. Bianchi (ed.), *Cleopatra's Egypt: Age of the Ptolemies*. Brooklyn: Brooklyn Museum, 1988.

R.S. Bianchi, 'Not the Isis Knot', *BES* 2, 1980: 9–31.

J. Quaegebeur, 'Cleopatra VII and the cults of the Ptolemaic queens', in R.S. Bianchi (ed.) *Cleopatra's Egypt: Age of the Ptolemies*. Brooklyn: Brooklyn Museum, 1988: 41–54.

J. Quaegebeur, 'The Egyptian clergy and the cult of the Ptolemaic dynasty.' *AS* 20, 1989: 93–116.

P.M. Fraser, *Ptolemaic Alexandria*. Oxford: Oxford University Press, 1972; reprinted 1998.

R.R.R. Smith, *Hellenistic Royal Portraits*. Oxford: Oxford University Press, 1988; reprinted 1998.

D. Svenson, 'Darstellungen Hellenistischer Könige mit Götterattributen', *Archäologische Studien*, Band 10. Frankfurt, 1995.

D.B. Thompson, *Ptolemaic Oinochoai and Portraits in Faience, Aspects of the Ruler-Cult*. Oxford: Oxford University Press, 1973.

S. Walker and P. Higgs, *Cleopatra of Egypt: From History to Myth*. London: British Museum Press, 2001.

S. Wilkinson, *Modern Egypt and Thebes*, vol. 1. London: John Murray, 1843.

Chapter 7

D. Arnold, *Temples of the Last Pharaohs*. New York: Oxford University Press, 1999.

F. Dunand, *Le culte du Isis dans le basin oriental de la Méditerranée*. Leiden: E.J. Brill, 1973.

H. Lavagne, *Hadrien Trésors d'une villa impériale*. Milan: Electa, 1999.

K. Lembke, 'Das Iseum Campense in Rom. Studie über den Isis Kult unter Domitian', *Archäologische und Geschichte*, Band 3. Heidelberg, 1994.

W.L. MacDonald and J.A. Pinto, *Hadrian's Villa and its Legacy*. New Haven: Yale University Press, 1995.

H.W. Müller, *Il Culto di Iside Nell'Antica Benvento. Catalogo delle Sculture Provienienti dai Santuari Egiziani dell'Antica Benevento nel Museo del Sannio*. Benevento: Saggi e Studi del Museo del Sannio Biblioteca e Archivio Storico Provinciali di Benevento, 1971.

A. Roullet, *The Egyptian and Egyptianising Monuments of Imperial Rome*. Leiden: E.J. Brill, 1972.

S.A. Takács, *Isis and Sarapis in the Roman World*. Leiden: E.J. Brill, 1994.

Index